DISCOVERING
ARCHAEOLOGY

DISCOVERING
ARCHAEOLOGY
by Iris Barry

Longman Group Limited
Longman House
Burnt Mill, Harlow, Essex.

First published in Great Britain 1980

Created, designed and produced by
Trewin Copplestone Books Ltd, London.

Phototypeset by SX Composing Limited, Rayleigh, Essex.

Printed in Italy by New Interlitho, Milan.

British Library Cataloguing in Publication Data
Barry, Iris
    Discovering archaeology.
    1. Archaeology – Juvenile literature
    I. Title
    930'. 1   CC171

ISBN 0-582-39091-5

Contents

The World of Archaeology

Archaeology begins the moment we throw something away – the empty medicine bottle, the broken necklace, the cracked pot. It is always beginning as time and people move on, leaving behind material remains. At its farthest it touches the gradual development of human beings from their ape-like ancestors. At its closest it is about the things which were used only yesterday.

Archaeologists discover and explore the tombs of long-dead Chinese rulers, or try to work out what Stone Age people had for dinner. They try to decipher the writings of those who lived three thousand years ago, and study how nineteenth century weaving machines work. Archaeologists dig in places as different from each other as the Arctic tundra, the deserts of the Sahara and the swamps of New Guinea. Some excavate lost cities. Others carefully search for the discarded fish bones and flint chippings left by people who lived and died before the use of metal. These are the clues that archaeologists use to reconstruct the past. They are detectives of a past that has shaped us all.

Some are proud to be known as 'dirt archaeologists' – those who set out trenches across a site and get down on their knees to clear away the earth from a fragment of bone or pot. Others are more at home in a laboratory or feeding hundreds of figures into a carefully programmed computer. The methods they use vary enormously. But all of them are dedicated to rescuing and preserving for us and for future generations what would otherwise be destroyed by the onrush of time, or lie forever hidden in the earth.

This book is about archaeology and archaeologists. It shows something of the variety of the subject, and explains how archaeologists work to make the clock run backwards so that we may look once more on the long vanished past.

In this book we have used the ancient names, where they are known, that archaeologists use, for the sites and civilizations that they investigate. The modern names are also given to help you locate these places and peoples.

The First Archaeologists

People have always marvelled at ruins from the past, explaining them away as the works of gods or giants. It was in the mid-fifteenth century that interest in the study of antiquity arose. By the sixteenth and seventeenth centuries, scholars in Europe had begun to take the examination and recording of these remains seriously and to theorize about them. When the Americas and Africa were being explored, Europeans came into contact with unfamiliar peoples and ways of life which could only be explained by looking at the past.

The early archaeologists, or Antiquarians as they called themselves, had no way of dating most of the ruins they studied, as there were no written records. They looked for their explanations in the literature and learning of the classical world of the ancient Greeks and Romans, and in the story of the Creation in the Old Testament. However, knowledge of the past grew steadily during the seventeenth and eighteenth centuries when excavations began to be carried out. Digging for treasure in ancient burial mounds and graves became a hobby for the educated classes. Stone implements dug from the ground were recognized as the tools of our early ancestors, very like those used by native peoples in the Americas or Africa. Some of these tools were found in the same layers of soil as the bones of extinct mammals.

Unfortunately, the study of the distant past was hindered by the accepted view that the world had been created in 4004 BC. Scholars did not know how literally to take the Biblical accounts of the early history of the world, or how to fit the increasing number of archaeological remains they knew about into such a short span of time. Also, they could not say how old the remains were, unless they contained datable inscriptions or coins.

During the eighteenth century, scientists began to study geology and examine the fossil remains which were found in some rocks. Many realized that the strata of the Earth, the layers of different sorts of rocks and soils, showed the order in which these had been laid down. By studying stratification the history of the Earth might be revealed. But how could they explain the finds of the fossilized bones of extinct creatures? It was becoming more and more difficult to believe that the Earth was just a few thousand years old!

By the end of the eighteenth century, excavation techniques were becoming more advanced, and excavators were seriously looking for evidence which would throw light on our past. When J. C. Thomsen tried to organize the national museum collection of Denmark, he saw that there was an order into which remains could be placed. He suggested that all artefacts, or things made by human beings,

During the eighteenth and nineteenth centuries, many ancient burial mounds were excavated by antiquarians and early archaeologists. Not all were as careful as this team working in the Mississippi valley.

The Aztecs of Mexico decorated this human skull with turquoise mosaic. Their craftsmanship astounded sixteenth century artists and scholars in Europe.

In England, early in the nineteenth century, Sir Charles Lyell argued that the world had been formed and was still forming by slow, gradual processes. The Earth was very old and life had existed on it for millions of years. In France, Boucher de Perthes found stone tools together with the bones of extinct animals in the gravel beds of the Somme. He published these discoveries as further evidence of the great antiquity of the human race. The public would not accept these amazing views.

Charles Darwin's theories also met with fierce opposition. He combined all the evidence collected so far with his own observations of living creatures. He suggested that new species evolved by the survival of those best adapted to the conditions under which they lived. In this way the human race had emerged from nature. There was no longer a place for God's direct intervention in the process of our creation. During the latter part of the nineteenth century, these ideas were accepted and the study of archaeology grew rapidly. The way was now clear for a more scientific approach. In Dorset, General Pitt Rivers organized huge excavations with military precision, and invented many of the methods of excavation we use today. Since his time archaeologists, equipped with the latest scientific techniques, have travelled the world in their quest for our buried past.

recovered from the ground could be arranged by the three materials used successively, and related to one of three 'Ages': the Stone, Bronze and Iron Ages. Now finds could be placed in order and linked to particular types of society.

Workmen excavate a ditch with military precision for General Pitt-Rivers at South Lodge, Dorset, 1893.

Discovering Early Civilizations

While other archaeologists were slowly proving that people had existed for hundreds of thousands of years before civilization, a few pioneer archaeologists were uncovering the riches that existed at the dim beginnings of history. During the nineteenth and early twentieth centuries they rediscovered civilizations which had been lost but not forgotten. They were not discouraged by difficult working conditions or the size of the task they had set themselves. These men revealed ancient cities and lost treasures which stirred the imagination of the world.

One of the first of these discoverers to capture the public's attention was Austen Henry Layard, who dug in the Middle East in the 1840s. Layard worked at Nimrud and Nineveh in Mesopotamia (part of modern Iraq), cities mentioned in the Bible. At both sites he made important discoveries. At Nineveh, he unearthed vast palaces and

Gold mask from a grave at Mycenae. Schliemann believed it portrayed King Agamemnon himself.

found the great library of King Sennacherib, who reigned from 704 to 681 BC. The library was made up of over 25 000 clay tablets inscribed with cuneiform, or wedge-shaped, writing. Some told stories of gods and heroes. Others revealed details of plant life, herbal cures for many illnesses

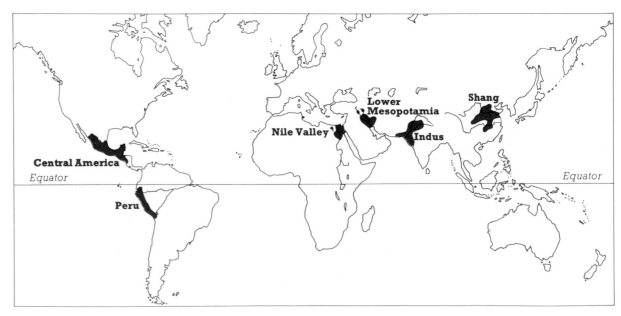

The most important centres of ancient civilizations date from about 3000 BC to AD 1500. The earliest civilizations developed first in Mesopotamia and later in the Nile Valley. The Indus and Shang civilizations followed a little later. In the Americas cities developed much later about AD 300–1500.

High in the Andes mountains of Peru, the abandoned Inca citadel of Machu Picchu lay forgotten for nearly 400 years, until it was rediscovered by Hiram Bingham.

and observations of the stars. Layard's discoveries received enormous publicity. With great difficulty he transported some of his most impressive discoveries to London, such as the huge human-headed stone bulls from Nimrud. This preserved them for the future and whetted the public appetite.

The next great discovery was made by a retired German trader and banker, Heinrich Schliemann, who began excavating in 1870 on the west coast of Turkey. Schliemann had long believed that the Greek poet Homer's description of the wars between Greeks and Trojans in the *Iliad* and the *Odyssey* was based on a true story. The Greeks besieged the city of Troy because Paris, son of King Priam, had stolen Helen, the beautiful wife of a Greek king. In a few seasons' work, Schliemann was able to prove that Troy lay hidden beneath the mound at Hissarlik, and that he had found the city of King Priam. Schliemann also used Homer to explain what he found. When he discovered a great hoard of golden jewellery, he believed he had found the treasure of the slain King Priam. In 1876 he dug at Mycenae, legendary home of the Greek warrior-king, Agamemnon, who had fought against the Trojans. Schliemann found six graves containing the fabulous funeral treasure of a very rich royal family. He claimed that one piece, a mask, showed the face of Agamemnon himself. Many of Schliemann's conclusions and dates are now known to be wrong. There had been several cities of Troy, each built upon the ruins of

the last, and he had dug too deep. But his work has been valuable to archaeologists, for it revealed a civilization that nobody believed had existed.

The task of excavating Knossos on Crete fell to Arthur Evans. This was the site of the Labyrinth, or maze, where legend told of youths and maidens sacrificed to a monster – half man, half bull – the Minotaur. Starting in 1897 Evans revealed the remains of a vast and complex palace, which he interpreted as the palace of King Minos, whose wife was mother of the Minotaur. Its many rooms and wall-paintings of youths vaulting over the horns of charging bulls were evidence of the Labyrinth and the legend that had grown up around it.

Amazing discoveries were also being made in the Americas. Explorers began to find, map and record the remains of the Aztec and Inca civilizations. They identified long-forgotten cities and ceremonial centres. The dense jungles of Central America were penetrated, and the first pictures drawn of the ruins of the most fascinating of these ancient civilizations, the Maya. Inscriptions have been found which reveal their advanced knowledge of mathematics and astronomy. But the ruins of huge stone pyramids and scattered cities are all that remain of this great civilization which disappeared mysteriously over a thousand years ago. Further south, Hiram Bingham climbed the Andes of Peru, in 1911, to discover the 'lost city of the Incas', Machu Picchu.

Archaeology from the Air

During the First World War, photographs of the ground were taken from aircraft for military purposes. By accident it was noticed that many of these photographs revealed archaeological features which could not be seen at ground level. The outlines of buildings buried beneath the soil, the patterns of drainage ditches which had not been used for a long time and the layouts of old areas of cultivation were all shown clearly on photographs. Since that time, the use of air photography in archaeology has developed to the point where it is, in many parts of the world, the most important method of discovering and mapping new sites.

Archaeological remains show up from the air in several ways. Slight hollows or mounds caused, for example, by the remains of old ditches, irrigation channels, earthworks or barrows (burial mounds), may be emphasized in the shadows cast by the Sun when it is low in the sky in the early morning or towards sunset. Photographs taken at this time of day can capture these give-away shadow patterns

Infra-red photography shows up archaeological remains, such as ploughed-out Bronze Age burial mounds, otherwise invisible to us.

Melting snow and low-angled rays from the setting Sun reveal an Iron Age hillfort in Devon.

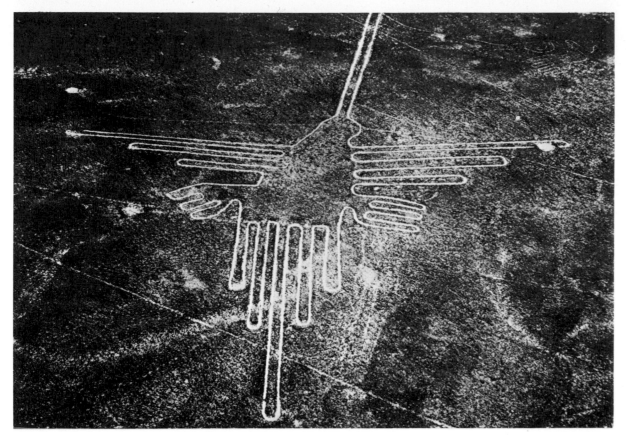

Huge drawings of abstract shapes and animals, such as this humming-bird, were made before AD 600 in the coastal desert of Peru. It is a mystery how the Nazca people set out these designs, which can only be appreciated from the air.

which, from the ground, do not seem significant.

Buried remains, or traces of earlier human activity now beneath the soil, can affect the growth of plant life above them for thousands of years. Vegetation grows strongly or poorly according to the moisture which reaches its roots. Plants growing above buried masonry and buildings receive less water than those over ordinary soil. Those growing on top of old ditches or pits flourish in the damp soil in these areas. These differences lead to weak or strong growth and reveal themselves in 'crop marks'. These are lines of lighter or darker vegetation, thicker or thinner growth. They can be seen and photographed from the air. Marks in the colour of the top-soil in an area can reveal disturbances caused by building, ploughing or ditching many centuries before. Even the way in which snow or frost melts, or dew settles on the soil, may show up buried walls or other patterns of soil disturbances which cause temperature differences at the surface. By carefully choosing the time of day and the season of the year, and by rephotographing the same area under different growth and weather conditions, archaeologists can build up a complete picture of a site in a way which it would be impossible

to do from ground level. Only when this has been done may they decide to excavate.

Air photography, especially with stereographic cameras which produce a three-dimensional effect, can also be of great help in surveying and mapping large sites and the areas in which they are situated. In recent years infra-red photography has been widely used. This can detect small changes in the temperature of the land surface which are caused by the presence of hidden remains beneath it. Although it is normal to use aircraft with either fixed 'mapping' cameras or hand-held ones, some archaeologists have ingeniously suspended cameras beneath balloons or kites. This is a cheaper but, of course, also a less controlled form of operation.

At the other extreme, photography by Earth satellites is likely to become very important in future years. Satellites can cover every area of the globe. Their sophisticated cameras can now produce pictures almost as good as those taken by low flying aircraft. Satellite photography, using infra-red and other radiation bands invisible to the human eye, will soon be used to detect archaeological remains beneath the sea or hidden under dense forest cover.

Prospecting for the Past

Before archaeologists put their spades into the ground, they must know what kind of site they are about to excavate and work out how they are going to do it. Once they have found a promising site, they set out to learn everything they can about it. As a first stage they study its position in the surrounding countryside. They work out how it fits in with local geology and geomorphology (the study of how the landscape was formed), water supplies and other resources. Next they study the surface of the site, looking for potsherds (which are pieces of broken pottery), stone chippings or any other signs of what lies beneath the ground. In some cases, the way vegetation grows thickly or poorly can show disturbances under the soil and hidden buildings. Earlier finds preserved in local museums or private collections may add useful knowledge of a site before it is dug.

Once this research has been done, archaeologists try to build up a picture of what lies underground and where the important areas are likely to be. Only when they have done this will they feel it is safe to begin digging. Sometimes it is possible to identify the best places to dig by fairly simple methods. The ground can be probed with a long steel rod. If it meets an obstacle, hard floors or living areas, for example, may be suspected. Major features, such as walls, can be picked out and mapped in this way. The

depth of the remains below the surface can be checked with a hollow drill or auger.

These simple methods of probing and augering take time and can destroy or damage objects. One way of preventing this makes use of the fact that certain remains create small local changes in the Earth's magnetic field. Iron objects, fired clay such as pottery, hearths and ovens, some ditches and some types of walls, tombs and buildings, all give rise to variations. One way to detect these variations is by a proton magnetometer. The protons in hydrogen atoms are made to spin faster by stronger magnetic fields, such as those produced by buildings beneath the soil, and slower by weaker magnetic fields when there are no hidden remains. When a large number of hydrogen protons are affected in this way, the spinning can be shown as an alternating current in an electrical circuit. Changes in a magnetic field can, therefore, be measured as changes in an alternating current.

The first proton magnetometers were very simple. They were bottles of water, containing the hydrogen atoms, surrounded by many coils of thin wire connected to a dial. Now they are more complicated and sensitive. By taking a proton magnetometer over a site, archaeologists can very quickly build up an accurate map of many underground remains. If they are not careful however,

Thousands of Etruscan tombs have been discovered by using a resistivity meter.

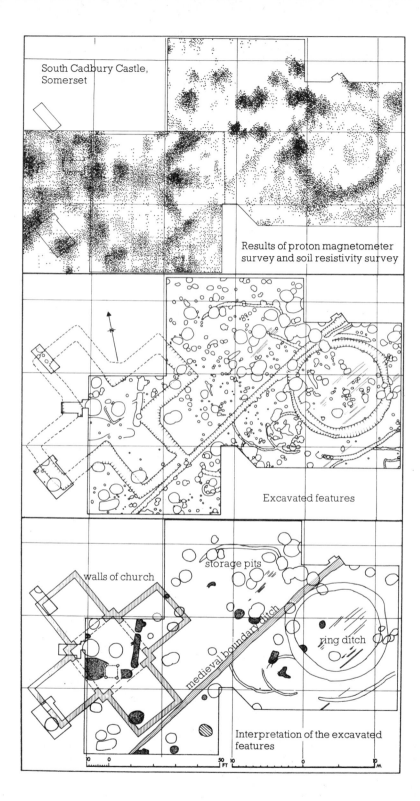

South Cadbury Castle, Somerset

Results of proton magnetometer survey and soil resistivity survey

Excavated features

walls of church

storage pits

medieval boundary ditch

ring ditch

Interpretation of the excavated features

A geophysical survey at South Cadbury, Dorset, gave a preview of features of this multi-period site before excavation.

Geophysical surveying at South Cadbury, which was possibly the seat of the legendary King Arthur.

they can as easily be led to a modern sewer system as to a Roman irrigation channel two thousand years old!

Another method of prospecting makes use of the way disturbances in the soil, such as buildings, pits and ditches, produce differing degrees of resistance to the passage of an electrical current. The soil above tombs, walls and floors is drier than undisturbed soil and gives a higher resistance reading. Filled-in pits and ditches are damper and give lower resistance than undisturbed soil. A simple form of soil resistivity meter can be made by pushing two metal rods into the ground, connecting a battery across them, and measuring the ratio of the voltage to the current which passes between them. A graph can then be plotted which will show the extremes of resistance, and the archaeologist can excavate in these places.

Modern resistivity meters are far more elaborate but they use the same principle. They are particularly useful in areas where proton magnetometers do not work well, such as those near the magnetic fields set up by power lines. Resistivity surveying has been very useful in finding large numbers of remains quickly. In Italy it was used to pinpoint over ten thousand Etruscan graves and tomb chambers. Little is known about the Etruscans, who were conquered by the Romans over 2000 years ago. Their civilization and language were completely destroyed.

The basic method of resistivity surveying has now been developed so that a computer can almost instantly process any changes detected in the soil's resistivity, and draw a map of these.

Excavation:1

Excavation lies at the heart of archaeology. It provides the archaeologist with the hard facts that are used to check and improve theories and to reconstruct the past. But excavation is expensive and time consuming. More important, it is destructive. It is only carried out when it is absolutely necessary. Perhaps there is no other way to answer certain questions. Sometimes a site is threatened by motorway construction or natural forces, such as floods or cliff fall. Excavation is only carried out after thorough preliminary investigation.

Geologists in the eighteenth century had shown how important stratification was in revealing the way the Earth had developed, and in helping them date particular layers. Stratification is the way in which rocks and soils in the Earth form visible layers, the most recent ones lying on top of the earlier ones. Later archaeologists realized the importance of stratification when it happened on a smaller scale, such as when a group of people inhabited a cave year after year and dropped household rubbish in it, when a grave was filled in, or when one house was built on top of the remains of another. By slicing carefully through the earth, archaeologists could reveal these strata and the objects embedded in them. Each layer, usually of a different colour or texture, represents a definite period in the use of that site. Often the depth of the layer can show the length of that period. By identifying and linking the same layers in different areas of a site, archaeologists can prove that different objects found in those strata belong to the same period.

The aim of an excavation is not just to dig up ancient coins or to expose mosaic pavements. It is also to connect finds with particular layers which will show the order in which things happened on that site. Sometimes a whole site is excavated with layer after layer carefully removed. This is, of course, expensive and usually kept for small structures such as huts and burial mounds. At other times digging is kept to a small area, which is either stripped or has rectangular trenches set out across it.

The first stage of excavation is sheer hard work. Many sites, especially in old towns, are covered by several metres of rubble and old foundations which must be removed before the real work can begin. In country areas

Archaeologists use earth-moving machinery to remove modern foundations, before they can excavate ancient levels.

Every find and feature is carefully plotted on scale drawings of the site. Portable one metre square grids, with internal strings forming ten centimetre subdivisions, help the archaeologist transfer information accurately from the soil to graph paper.

Checks on the stratigraphy are made throughout the excavation, as layers are removed and new features discovered.

sites are often covered by permanent pasture or by deep plough-soil, both of which can be stripped off down to the archaeological deposits. Earth-moving machinery and picks and shovels are the tools used in these operations. It is only much later that the delicate excavation work, which most people imagine archaeologists doing, comes into the picture.

The site is surveyed and fixed on the best large-scale published map of the area. The director of the excavation must be able to record the exact position, in three dimensions, of anything on the site. Using wooden stakes, nails and string, an accurately measured grid is laid out. Each square marked off has its own reference number, and finds from each square are drawn onto a plan. As the archaeologist digs down into the site, the successive layers

which are uncovered in the vertical trench walls are also carefully drawn to scale on graph paper. These plans and section drawings are as important a part of the evidence as the photographs and finds themselves.

As archaeologists work they destroy much of their evidence. They disturb and remove layers, carry away excavated soil to a waste or spoil heap, and take away finds and soil samples for further study. After the excavation the only evidence which will remain is that in notebooks, drawings and photographs and, of course, the finds themselves. Archaeologists, therefore, record everything they do and every aspect of the site. A single seed could tell them that early farmers were cultivating maize long before it was thought likely. The reddish colour of burnt earth could lead them to the hearth of an Iron Age hut.

Excavation: 2

Now the really painstaking work begins. Trowels, small brushes and tiny dental tools take the place of picks and shovels. The earth is gently removed from around finds and delicate items are photographed in position. They are often reinforced with polyvinyl acetate solution, which is painted on and hardens quickly, or by bandaging the object and pouring plaster of paris around it to make a hard shell. All the excavated earth is sifted through a bank of sieves with graduated meshes to make sure that even the smallest items, such as beads and fish bones, are found. Photographs in colour and black and white are taken at every stage and in different kinds of light.

Details of pottery shapes and decoration are often shown more clearly in drawings than in photographs.

A fine spray of water is often the best way to excavate fragile bones.

Thousands of potsherds must be sorted and studied before the detailed history of a site, its date and trading connections can be worked out.

Pieces of pottery, bone and worked stone, which need no laboratory treatment, are put in trays or bags labelled with the site name-code, year and layer number. Each excavator has a special tray for the things he or she finds while digging, and must be careful to keep finds from one layer separate from those of the next. At the end of the day, find-trays are taken to the finds shed, where the potsherds are washed, dried and marked with the code in indian ink. Small finds, such as coins, glass, brooches and knife-blades, are numbered and treated separately. Each is usually measured in accurately on the horizontal grid and marked on the plan. A detailed diary is kept covering all aspects of the dig.

Modern excavation is a matter of teamwork. It often involves several specialists, for example an animal bone expert or a specialist in recovering and identifying ancient plant remains. The work can only be done properly if the director and site foreman have complete control over what is done. The excavators themselves must know exactly what they are expected to do and how their particular tasks and finds fit into the jigsaw puzzle of the whole excavation. Digging is hard work. It is tiring spending all day perhaps knee-deep in mud, scrubbing potsherds or sieving excavated soil. But the occasional reward of unearthing a bronze brooch, or the thrill of finding a wall-painting, compensates for all the drudgery.

Preserving Our Past

It is very important to preserve ancient objects after they have been excavated, so that they do not crumble or decay any further. They are usually sent to a laboratory to be repaired and restored by highly trained staff. First, however, the excavator is responsible for making sure that finds are treated immediately, so that they reach the laboratory in the best possible state. Fragile material must be supported and strengthened before or immediately after it is removed from the soil. This may be done by treating it with wax or a solution containing plastic, or by building up a support around it with plaster, cloth or paper. Wood which has absorbed water becomes soft, heavy and weakened. It must not be allowed to break under its own weight, or to dry out, as it will then crack and distort. It is usually wrapped and kept damp or kept underwater.

When an object has been excavated its condition will depend on a number of things. The most important are the materials of which it is made, the surrounding soil and the length of time it has been buried. In most soil conditions organic materials disappear completely. These are materials which have been obtained from living organisms,

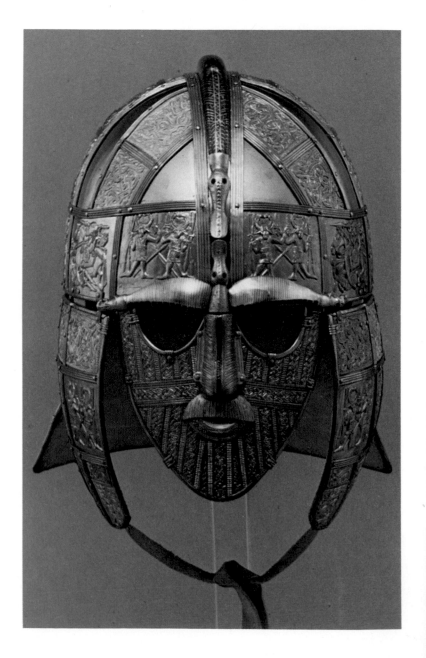

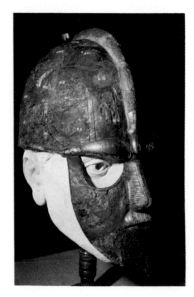

The Sutton Hoo helmet, made in Sweden, was found broken and distorted in the soil. The first reconstruction (right) was made soon after the helmet's discovery. The second reconstruction (far right) is much more accurate.

such as wood, paper and leather. A buried ship, carrying the funeral treasure of a seventh century Anglo-Saxon king, was discovered at Sutton Hoo, Suffolk. The wood of which it was made had vanished but impressions, stains and nails in the soil showed where it had been. On the other hand, organic materials can last well in dry conditions. The hot, dry climate in Egypt has preserved the feather fans and wooden cosmetic boxes of noble ladies who died four thousand years ago. In very damp soil, clay and bone soon become fragile and may fall apart if not carefully dried.

The laboratory treatment of wood from archaeological sites is now highly developed. The main purpose is to replace any water which has been absorbed into the timber by another substance which will not damage it. This will strengthen it and prevent the remains from changing shape. The most popular way of doing this is by allowing the wood to slowly absorb polyethylene glycol, a type of wax. Many archaeological specimens, when recovered, contain chemicals in solution which can harm them, especially if crystallization occurs later. In some materials, such as ivory, bone or stone, these chemicals can be removed by careful washing. Unbaked clay remains, such as cuneiform tablets or waterlogged pottery, are carefully dried in the laboratory and can then be baked. This may change their appearance but it preserves them for study. Metal objects frequently suffer in the soil. They may become corroded or, in extreme cases, all the original metal may be changed into another substance. X-ray examination may reveal the shape of the original object and details of how it was made. Deposits caused by corrosion can be removed by chemical and mechanical methods.

Once an object has been treated to stop it decaying it must be stored safely. Most objects must be kept in surroundings of a dry, even temperature. Ultra-violet light must be kept from textiles which it would fade. The most

fragile items may need to be strengthened. This is often done by treating them with special resins, sometimes in a vacuum, to make sure that the strengthening material penetrates as deeply as possible. Objects are usually restored in such a way that the process can be easily reversed. The restored parts are carefully made so that they cannot be confused with the genuine pieces. This system allowed the king's helmet in the Sutton Hoo ship burial to be reconstructed twice, when it was realized that the first reconstruction was incorrect.

Piecing together the three-dimensional jigsaw puzzle of a broken pot is more difficult than it looks. Sherds are often missing, and the smallest mistake can throw the whole vessel askew.

Remains from the Earth

Most of an archaeologist's finds are objects made from inorganic, or lifeless, material, such as metal, stone, glass or pottery. This is because these materials last longer than organic ones. Many scientific techniques have been developed to examine these materials so that they will give up the secrets of their age, origin and use.

Stone tools are the main evidence of the activities of our most ancient ancestors. Sometimes only the tools are found but occasionally excavators find the sites where they were made. By examining the amount of waste and rejected material at such sites, the way it is scattered and perhaps by trying to make similar tools themselves, they may learn something of the time and effort involved in tool making. On a few sites, like the vast flint mines at Grimes Graves in Norfolk, excavators may also be able to work out how many people were involved in producing the essential raw material.

Archaeologists can establish how a tool was used and what it was used on by examining, under a microscope, the patterns of wear on its edges or point. The origins of a stone artefact can be traced by taking a very thin, translucent slice from it to examine under a microscope. This reveals the characteristic features of the rock from which it was made. These can then be compared with those of material from known sites. In this way carved jade ornaments of the Maya civilization of Central America (AD 300–900) have been traced to particular jade sources, and trading contacts over the whole of Central America have been revealed.

Pottery is the most common material discovered by archaeologists. It can be dated successfully in modern laboratories. Also, by careful study of its shape and structure and the material from which it is made, a great deal can be discovered about the techniques used to make it and its connection with pottery from other sites. The main ingredients in the clay used can be revealed under a microscope and these can be confirmed by spectrometry. This entails vapourizing samples of the clay, so that the

This carved jade plaque was found in Highland Mexico.

Maya sites in Central America. Precious apple-green jade was traded hundreds of kilometres from its source in the Motagua River, Guatemala, to great Maya cities such as Tikal and Uxmal.

This corroded, shapeless lump of metal was found in a grave in southern England.

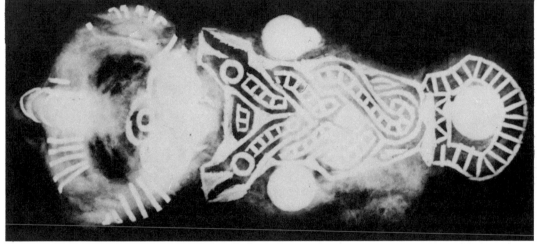

When X-rayed, it proved to be an inlaid Anglo-Saxon buckle.

particular wavelengths of light given out by each element in it can be recorded. Each element has its own wavelength which identifies it immediately. Some kinds of Japanese and Chinese pottery have been studied using this method. Although there were many beautiful vases in museums, no one knew exactly from where they came. Now this has been worked out by comparing the clay they were made from with potsherds from excavations in the Far East.

Metal objects are often corroded and may have to be X-rayed to reveal their original shapes. Faults or joins may show up which suggest how they were made. The structure of a metal object, how it was made and how it was allowed to cool, can be revealed by polishing a small area, etching this with acid and examining it under a microscope. X-rays and spectrometry are used to identify the elements present in a metal so that the ore they originally came from can be traced. Many careful examinations must be made in a laboratory to build up a picture of the changes in metal working in the distant past.

About four thousand years ago, the Beaker people migrated from western Europe to the British Isles. They used short, flat daggers made of almost pure copper. These were such precious possessions that their owners were buried with them. Later the Wessex people learnt to make bronze. This is an alloy of tin and copper and is hard and long-lasting. We know that they put the ideal twelve per cent of tin into their beautiful tapering daggers, which greatly improved their strength.

Obsidian, a volcanic glass, was one inorganic material which was traded widely in the distant past. It was used for making razor sharp blades and spear and arrow heads. In recent years, archaeologists have tried to date obsidian artefacts by making use of the fact that a freshly-made obsidian surface will slowly take up water from its surroundings. This makes a layer that can be measured so that the age of the artefact can be worked out fairly accurately. Chemical and other analyses of obsidian can indicate where it came from. This has helped to build up a picture of ancient trade routes.

Clues from Plants

Plant foods have always been an important part of the human diet, although not many human groups have ever been entirely vegetarian. Plants and trees are also used by people for many other purposes, such as for clothing, building, weapons, basketry and dyes. Vegetable material rots quickly in most conditions. Yet in some others, such as peat bogs or very dry places, it survives for thousands of years. Where it is preserved, it can throw light not only on what our ancestors ate but also on what they did. Most important of all, perhaps, it can tell us about the environment in which all this took place and how, over time, our ancestors changed their surroundings.

Plant remains do not just provide clues to the diet of earlier peoples. They also tell us whether they were collecting wild or growing domesticated plants, or even how far they roamed to get their food. The remains of food from plants are preserved in many ways. In Egypt, dried seeds have been recovered from tombs and storage pits, and from the intestines of mummies. Coprolites (fossilized or dried faeces) also contain undigested parts of food plants

which can be identified. Dried coprolites were examined from the site at Huaca Prieta on the desert coast of Peru. It seems that the inhabitants, who lived there four thousand years ago, ate mainly beans, squash (pumpkin) and starchy roots, with some mussels and small sea creatures, such as crabs, for delicacies. Burnt seeds are sometimes preserved in a carbonized form or leave their impressions in pottery or bricks. Occasionally, actual items of food are found which contain recognizable grains like wheat and barley.

Plant remains also provide us with other evidence, such as the time of year at which a particular site was used. A large number of peach stones found on an excavation would hint that the site was inhabited during the months of May and June. Contact between various places can be proved as, for example, when maize and tobacco were introduced into Africa from the Americas in the early sixteenth century.

Recovering plant remains is now an essential part of excavation. You can sometimes identify large seeds or the shells of nuts by the naked eye, but often vegetable

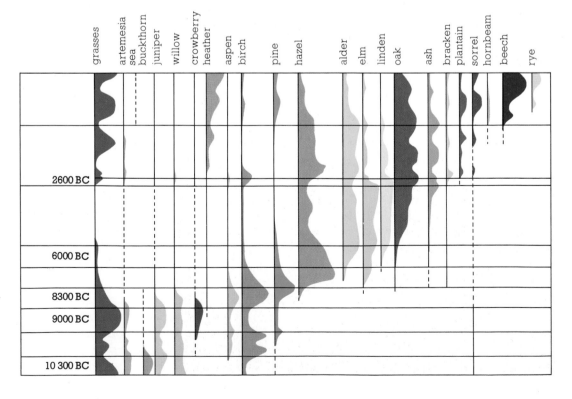

Analysis of pollen samples taken from different layers of an archaeological site can build up a picture of what was growing in the area thousands of years ago, and how the vegetation was affected by human activity. This pollen diagram shows vegetational changes in Jutland, Denmark.

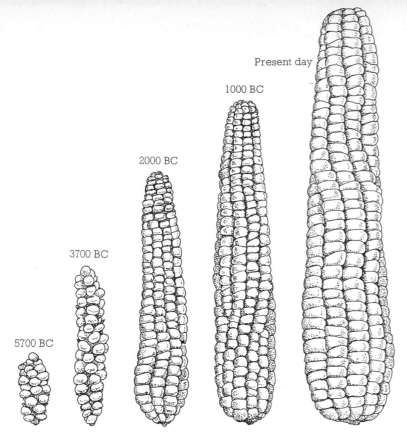

5700 BC 3700 BC 2000 BC 1000 BC Present day

In the Tehuacan valley, Mexico, archaeologists have found evidence of the prehistoric domestication of maize. The earliest type of maize cob found was a wild species. Later examples show that people were cultivating maize and gradually improving it by careful breeding. Here early types of maize are compared to a modern cob.

remains are too small for this. In recent years, archaeologists have developed ways of floating these, which are usually light, out of the soil of a site. This can be done by putting the dried soil in water, agitating it, and then scooping off what floats to the top to be examined later. This is done by a seed machine. It consists of a large tank containing water with a frothing agent, similar to washing-up liquid, and a bubbler unit which pumps air into the water, making it bubble. The seeds then float to the surface.

Each plant or tree produces its own particular form of pollen which can be identified under a microscope. This pollen is produced in large quantities and spreads out from the plant, often over a wide area. Luckily for the archaeologist it is the toughest part of the plant. By building up a picture of the types of pollen from a site or from one layer in a site, archaeologists can discover which trees and plants were growing in the area during the period when the site was occupied. By seeing how pollen types change over time, they can discover how the vegetation changed and work out how far this was due to human activity. For example, if tree pollens decline and pollens from grasses increase, then early farmers may have been clearing the forest to cultivate the land.

Other alterations can suggest vast changes in the climate and vegetation, for example, the coming of Ice Ages and the warmer periods that followed them. Pollen analysis can provide fascinating details about the past. The plants laid in the Sutton Hoo ship burial were proved, by pollen analysis, to be hazel, heather and ivy.

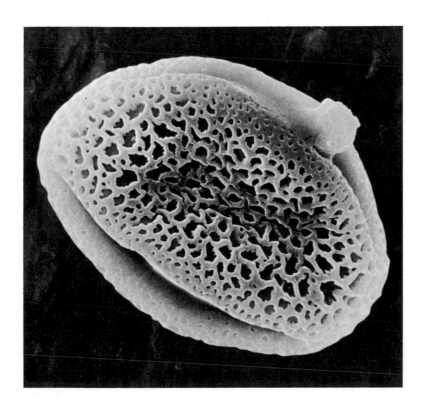

Every plant produces unique identifiable pollen grains. This pollen grain from a Scots Pine has been greatly magnified.

23

Digging up Bones

There is a grisly fascination about watching an excavator brush the soil away from a skeleton. Complete skeletons are not often found in excavations, but even fragments of bones can be made to reveal clues to the past.

Human bones find their way into the earth in many ways, some deliberate, some accidental. Bodies may be buried carefully in graves, tumbled into pits or fall accidentally down shafts. A corpse may be partly cremated and the bones then buried, or the flesh allowed to rot so the skull or jaw-bone can be kept as a trophy or memorial. Bones from one site may be swept away by a swollen stream and deposited in another, or carried off and damaged by wild animals. Animal bones may be buried in rubbish dumps, left behind by hunters after the meat has been butchered, or buried by rock falls.

The excavator's first job is to uncover the bones carefully in the earth. When these have been broken and jumbled this is not always easy. If they have become fossilized, the

The skull of an ancient Peruvian who survived dangerous operations on his head.

surrounding rock may have to be cut or dissolved away. Some may need to be strengthened before they are lifted. Damp, newly excavated bone will often harden if allowed to dry gently. Excavating skeletons is slow, painstaking work and archaeologists must record every bone.

This well-preserved corpse of a man who died about 2000 years ago was found in a bog at Tollund, Denmark. He wore a conical leather cap, and the tight noose around his neck shows that he was hanged. Analysis of his stomach contents showed that he had eaten porridge flavoured with herbs as his last meal.

24

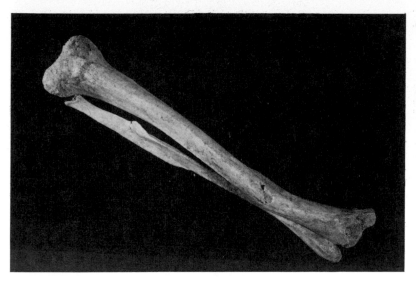

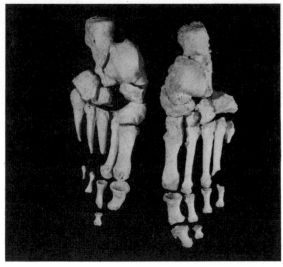

Bones can tell us about accidents and illnesses that befell their owners. Above is a spiral fracture of the lower leg.

These deformed bones show the crippling effects of leprosy on the feet.

Detective work begins as they try to work out from its position if a corpse was buried carefully or pushed hurriedly into a shallow hole. Were the fractures caused before or after death? In the pagan Anglo-Saxon period (AD 400–650) in England, women were sometimes buried alive with dead men. Archaeologists have found graves containing twisted female skeletons lying on top of male skeletons and pinned down by large rocks. Some skeletons may have been deliberately laid out in a particular direction, according to the custom of certain groups of people. For example, Christians traditionally were buried facing towards the east.

Bones which are not fossilized can be dated by measuring how much radioactive carbon they contain. The ages of bones which are found in the same cemetery can be checked against each other by the fluorine test. Most water contains fluorine which bones will absorb if they lie in damp soil long enough. By working out the amount of fluorine in bones from the same site, you can see if they were buried at the same time. This method was used to prove that Piltdown Man was a hoax. The discovery in Sussex, in 1912, of a skull and jaw-bone seemed to provide the missing link between human beings and our ape-like ancestors. However, the skull contained 0.1 per cent fluorine while the jaw-bone contained about 0.03 per cent fluorine. This showed that the jaw was much more recent than the skull.

Dating bones gives some idea of the age of a site. Close examination of human bones also tells us much about their former owners, their sex and at what age they died. Teeth not only reveal the age of the owners, but the way they have been worn down may suggest the type of food they ate. Dental decay increased rapidly when people became farmers and started eating more cereals. Damage to the bones may show what diseases they suffered from, such as tuberculosis, rickets and arthritis. Sometimes it is possible to decide what caused death. Spear or arrow heads are found still stuck fast in bones. Sword cuts to the skull, or the fractures caused by blows from clubs with star-shaped stone heads, leave clear marks. Occasionally, a skull may show that the owner was operated upon during his life. One Peruvian skull, about three thousand years old, shows that no less than seven discs of bone had been cut away. Bone had grown around the holes later, which proved that the victim had survived all these operations!

If several skeletons are found, it is possible to say something about the range of ages and number of men and women in a group of people. The shape of the body and particularly the skull can tell us about relationships with other groups.

There are usually more animal than human bones found on a site. By studying these, we can picture which animals were hunted for food and which were domesticated. Damage to the bones will show what methods the early hunters used to kill their prey and how they then butchered the meat.

The Carbon 14 Revolution

Dating finds is one of the archaeologist's greatest problems. It is sometimes possible to date finds of an unknown date when they are unearthed in the same layer as objects whose dates are known, such as coins. But some ancient societies produced no helpful landmarks of this sort, and for many years their ages and chronologies could only be estimated.

Many scientific techniques have been discovered during this century to date archaeological finds accurately. A revolution in dating happened in the 1940s. An American scientist, Willard Libby, showed that you could establish to within a fairly narrow time-margin the age of almost all organic materials, that is substances such as wood, charcoal, bone, flax, antler and peat, which were once part of living organisms. This could be done by working out how much of a particular sort of radioactive carbon was contained in these materials. This form of carbon is usually referred to as radiocarbon or carbon 14, to distinguish it from the more common, non-radioactive, carbon 12.

When plants are alive, they absorb carbon 14 and carbon 12 in more or less equal amounts from the atmosphere. Animals that eat the plants also absorb these two sorts of carbon. But when a living organism dies it no longer absorbs carbon. The carbon 14 already in its tissues or cells begins to decay or lose its radioactivity. The rate at which the decay occurs is known. After about 5730 years ± 40 years (the plus or minus gives room for error), about half the radioactivity is left. This is known as the 'half-life'. By measuring the proportion of carbon 14 to carbon 12 in any organic material, we can work out how much carbon 14 has disappeared since the organism died, and therefore how long ago its death occurred.

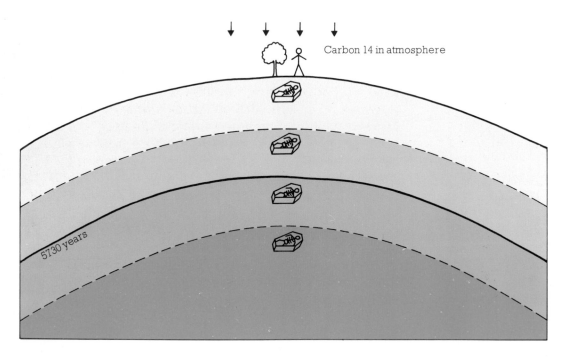

Carbon 14 in atmosphere

5730 years

Radioactive carbon is absorbed by all plants and animals. When they die, the carbon 14 stored in them begins to decay at a known rate. After 5730 years only half the radioactive carbon is left in them. Measurement of the radiocarbon content can therefore date accurately any organic material, such as wood and rope.

At Stonehenge, above, shallow carvings of daggers, seen below, on a massive vertical slab may date to the time of Mycenae, 3500 years ago, or they might be contemporary with nearby medieval graffiti.

Carbon 14 dating is usually expressed as plus or minus so many years BP, or 'Before Present', which is taken as 1950. A human bone, for example, may be dated as 2000 $\pm$ 100 BP, which would be 2100 to 1900 years before the present day. This would mean to us between 150 BC and AD 50. Therefore, by dating the archaeological find we can, with care, date the layer in which it was found.

Ideas about the pattern of our prehistory have been transformed by the revelations of radiocarbon dating. Many archaeological remains have been dated to periods far older than anyone had imagined. In Britain, it was long thought that the great circular monument at Stonehenge had been constructed in about 1600 BC by native barbarian tribes who were inspired by the early Greek civilization of Mycenae. The discovery of carvings of Mycenaean type daggers on one of the upright stones seemed to confirm this. But carbon 14 tests showed that the first monument built at Stonehenge, an earthen bank, was begun by 2500 BC and the stone circles were completed by 2000 BC. The civilization at Mycenae did not flower until about 1600 BC and so, even at this time, Stonehenge was an ancient monument. Perhaps the daggers were carved on the stone by a Mediterranean trader to mark his visit.

Unfortunately, the amount of carbon 14 present in the atmosphere, and available to be absorbed into living things, has varied over the years. This may have been due partly to changes in the Earth's magnetic field. The widespread burning of fossil fuels, such as coal and oil, in the last two centuries has reduced the amount of carbon 14 in the atmosphere, while the recent testing of atomic weapons has increased it. Research into radiocarbon dating is still going on throughout the world. Nevertheless, this method has given the archaeologist a tool of great power and many objects and sites have been securely dated by it.

Tree-ring Dating

This section through the trunk of an oak shows the annual rings.

Archaeologists are always seeking new, accurate ways to date the things they find. In the last sixty years, they have realized that the patterns of rings in timber may be of great help in fixing a date to archaeological sites in which wood is found.

As a tree grows, year by year distinctive rings form in its timber. These can be seen easily in a cross-section of a branch or the trunk. At the start of each growing season the tree produces a layer of large cells beneath its bark. As the season continues and winter draws near, these become smaller and smaller until growth almost stops. Then, with the next spring, large cells again begin to form. It is this continuous process which produces the characteristic pattern of concentric rings in a tree. It helps us to distinguish one year's growth from the next. But the pattern of growth is not the same in each year. In dry years, the tree will grow slowly and its annual growth ring will be thin, while wet years will be reflected in increased growth and thicker rings. The pattern of rings in a tree, therefore, gives a summary of the climate it has known in its lifetime.

Early this century, growth rings were studied in pieces of timber preserved in the dry areas of New Mexico and Arizona. It was soon noticed that different pieces showed the same pattern of rings. This led to the conclusion that they came from trees which had been alive at the same time, growing under the same conditions.

If we cut down a living tree, we can find out how old it is by counting the number of its rings inwards from the bark to the centre. The outermost ring represents the present year and the centre, the year of its first growth. Now if the tree rings show a recognizable patterning, for example two years of thin growth together occurring twenty-nine and thirty years ago (which indicate two years of dry weather), we can look for the same pattern in the rings of other trees. Suppose we found the same pattern in the last or outer two rings of one of those trees, we would know that that tree had died thirty years ago. By comparing the overlapping of distinctive growth ring patterns we can, with care and luck, construct a master pattern for growth rings going back many centuries. Archaeologists learnt to compare the pattern of growth rings in timber they had found in the old beams or posts of houses with the master

A sample is taken from a bristlecone pine and studied in the laboratory. Recognizable rings are marked for comparison with the master pattern.

pattern. They could then date the timber and so gain some idea of the age of the archaeological site. This method of dating is called dendrochronology.

However, there are certain complications in dating by this method. The pattern of growth rings varies if the trees are of different species and if they live in different environments. Where there are dramatic changes in temperature and rainfall over a short distance, ring patterns may vary greatly. Damage to a tree's top branches and leaves will also affect the cells it produces during a year.

To extend the master pattern back in history from trees alive now, there have to be examples of timber preserved from the past which overlap without a break. In northern Europe, the oak can live for up to five hundred years and

its wood is very long-lasting. It was often used in the construction of buildings and has provided the most useful set of ring patterns. But recently, the most important work has been done with the bristlecone pine. This tree grows at about 3000 metres in California and can live for over 1000 years. When it is dead, it is highly resistant to decay and damage by insects. From it scientists have now built up a master pattern of tree-rings dating back about 9000 years.

Radiocarbon dating can be checked against timber dated by dendrochronology. However, it is important to discover how long the timber had been dead before it was used and whether it had been re-used. There is no master pattern for areas where wood is scarce or where little is preserved because of a hot and humid climate.

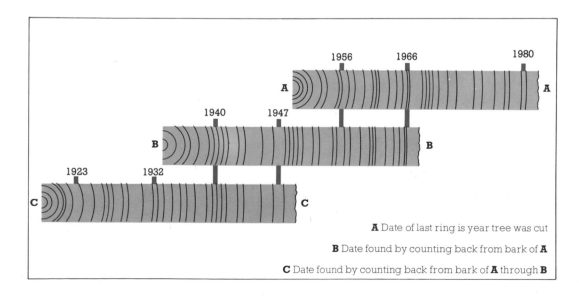

1956 1966 1980
A   A

1940 1947
B   B

1923 1932
C   C

A Date of last ring is year tree was cut

B Date found by counting back from bark of **A**

C Date found by counting back from bark of **A** through **B**

Annual growth rings can be identified and overlapped to make a master pattern extending into the past.

29

Other Dating Methods

The radiocarbon method can be used to date materials up to about 70 000 years old. However, the method becomes inaccurate as less and less carbon 14 remains in the object being examined. Another technique, the potassium-argon method (also based on radioactive decay), is used to date materials from very remote periods in history, as far back as ten million years ago. But it can only be used on volcanic rocks.

Potassium is one of the most common elements in the Earth's composition and a very small amount of it is radioactive. This potassium, potassium 40, decays at a known rate to produce calcium and the gas, argon 40. The half-life of potassium 40 is about 1.3 million years. Scientists can measure how much potassium 40 and argon 40 there are left in a piece of rock. They can then work out how long the potassium has been decaying and, therefore, how old the rock is. The older the rock, the more argon it will contain and the less potassium. The remains of the earliest hominids (Man-like creatures) were found embedded in layers of volcanic rock in the Rift Valley of East Africa. By dating each rock layer, the fossil remains were found to be over three million years old.

Potsherds are the most common archaeological find in most parts of the world. For many years, archaeologists compared pots, their shapes, surface decorations and the composition of the clay from which they were made, to decide from which period they came. But what was needed was some method whereby these pots could be dated absolutely, in calendar years. Pots are usually broken within a few years of being made, and so this would help them to date the layers in which potsherds were found.

In the last twenty years a method of doing this has been developed. This method, called thermoluminescence, depends on the fact that over time certain minerals trap extra electrons in the atoms which make up their crystals.

When the minerals are heated beyond a certain temperature, the electrons are freed and appear as light. Pottery is made from clay containing minerals, and when it is fired at about 700°C a pot is emptied of its trapped electrons. From that moment on it starts to age. Eventually, the pot is broken and thrown away. Over the years, as it lies buried in the ground, minute amounts of radioactive elements in and around it will produce new electrons which will become trapped in the fabric of the pot. The older the pot, the more electrons it will contain. It was discovered that if the pot were reheated after being unearthed, the electrons would be driven off in the form of light energy and this could be measured. In this way, the time since the pot was originally fired could be calculated.

Thermoluminescence has been used mainly to identify fakes. Some Greek statuettes and Peruvian pots, which came into museum collections over a hundred years ago, have recently proved to be copies of the real thing. Experimental research is still going on into this technique and it is a valuable check on radiocarbon dating.

Tests on potsherds from the deep cave system of the Cueva de los Tayos, in Ecuador, gave a date of 3450 ± 397 BP. This compared well with a radiocarbon date taken from sea-shells found in the same layer. The decorative sea-shells had been carried from the Pacific Ocean across the Andes and down into sacred caves in the Amazon jungle, possibly by pilgrims or traders, about 3000 years ago.

This diagram shows potassium-argon dating. Volcanic rocks contain radioactive potassium, which decays at a known rate. Measurement of the radioactivity can date layers millions of years old.

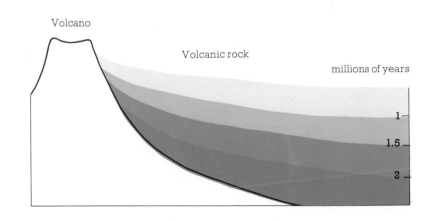

At Olduvai Gorge, Tanzania, early hominid remains were found. They were dated by the potassium-argon method.

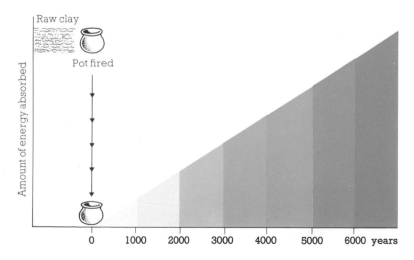

This diagram shows dating using thermoluminescence. Fired clay gradually absorbs electrons as it ages. Electrons can be measured as light energy, and an absolute date obtained.

31

Fakes and Frauds

There was great excitement among archaeologists in 1912. Charles Dawson, a country solicitor and amateur archaeologist, had found fragments of a skull, apparently of the same form as that of modern Man *(Homo sapiens)*, near to an ape-like jaw-bone and teeth. These were discovered near Piltdown, in Sussex. The 'ape' jaw fitted the human skull and the wear on the teeth indicated the creature had eaten a diet similar to that of humans. Nearby were found remains of extinct animals, dateable to about half a million years ago, and also some crude stone tools. The long sought-after 'missing link' between us and our ape-like ancestors seemed to have been found. More remarkable remains were found in the area in 1915, and eventually it was accepted that Piltdown Man was a most important early hominid.

It was not until 1953 that scientific dating techniques proved the whole thing was bogus. Radiocarbon tests showed that the skull was genuine but only about 50 000 years old. The jaw was from a modern ape and had been dyed, and the teeth had been filed down to the required shape and dyed. The fossil remains had been planted there to back up the supposed age of the skull. The whole affair was nothing but an ingenious hoax.

Who faked Piltdown Man is still uncertain. Perhaps it was done as a joke or to show how easily hoodwinked leading scientists could be. Or perhaps it was done to support a particular theory of evolution or to bring fame to the finder. No one really knows. The motive for other fakes is sometimes clearer. In North America, many fakes have been 'discovered' which seem to show that Phoenicians and Vikings from the Old World had travelled inland long before the time of Columbus and had erected inscribed stone monuments.

Archaeology and faking are almost inseparable. Sometimes real or fake material is inserted into an archaeological site to which it does not belong. This is called 'salting' and

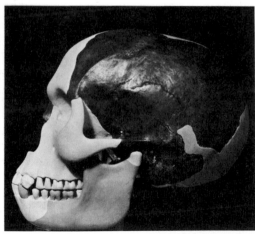

The Piltdown skull: the cranium (darker coloured) is human but the jaw is from an orang-utan and had been dyed to look convincing.

WORKERS AT PILTDOWN.

Excavators pose for the camera at Piltdown, Sussex.

This baked clay tablet from Glozel, France, is inscribed in an unknown script which has links with Latin, Phoenician and Iberian alphabets. Is it a fake or a genuine artefact?

Such works of art as this genuine Nok terracotta head can be tested by thermoluminescence and other scientific methods to show whether they are genuine or fakes.

goes back to Boucher de Perthes' excavations in France in the 1850s. There, the workmen, knowing visitors liked to see discoveries being made, planted genuine stone hand-axes and fossilized animal bones in places where they could hit upon them at promising moments.

During the 1920s many archaeologists became suspicious of the discoveries at Glozel in France. Here excavators claimed to have found items of Palaeolithic (Old Stone Age) art, as well as an unknown form of writing. Investigations on the spot suggested that someone was secretly burying fake material in the site and placing it in layers which suggested it had great age. The pieces looked like modern fakes and were ignored until a few years ago when thermoluminescence tests set their age at about 2000 years. The Glozel puzzle has taken on a new lease of life. Salting is usually noticeable. It is very hard to insert objects into layers in a way which cannot be spotted.

Another sort of faking is done to make money. The objects recovered by archaeologists are sometimes beautiful or rare. If they came on the market they would be easily sold to collectors or museums. The faker steps in to meet this demand. Such fakes are a great nuisance to archaeologists. If they are not spotted they may lead scholars to come to entirely wrong conclusions. In recent years, a number of fake terracotta (baked clay) human heads, in the style of the Nok culture of West Africa, have been reported. These are claimed to be about 2000 years old and to have been smuggled out of Nigeria. Their form is slightly different from true Nok pieces. If they were genuine, archaeologists would have to revise their ideas about the development of Nok art styles.

Fakes are easier to spot after a lapse of time. New scientific techniques are developed, or scholars learn more about the archaeology of the areas from which objects are supposed to come. When this happens the fakes begin to stand out. They do not fit in with genuine material and the scholar notices mistakes in their manufacture or design. If the suspected objects are closely examined, they will often show modern tool marks or evidence of manufacturing techniques unknown to the ancient craftsmen. Nevertheless, fakes and faking continue to be a hazard to the archaeologist.

Historical Archaeology

History begins with the existence of written documents. The time before writing was invented in any society is called prehistory. Much of archaeology is concerned with the prehistoric world. In Mesopotamia, which had one of the earliest civilizations, it is the period up to about five thousand years ago. In some other parts of the world, the prehistoric period lasted almost until the present day. Considering the three to four million years human beings have existed, all history is very recent.

Archaeologists have always made the best use they can of written records to understand what our ancestors thought and did. Inscriptions on Egyptian tombs, signs on Maya monuments, and royal proclamations made by Indian rulers such as Aśoka of the third century BC, have all thrown light on remains from those periods.

The decrees of Aśoka were inscribed on rock surfaces and specially erected pillars in places where people gathered. They were a sort of public notice. The writings explain the peaceful Buddhist ways which he wished his people to follow. They also list his good deeds.

'On the roads I have planted banyan trees, which will give shade to beasts and man. I have had many groves planted and I have had wells dug and rest houses built . . .

The archaeologist and the historian who studies our recorded past must have a good understanding of each other's needs when work on a site is progressing. Every possible piece of useful information needs to be extracted from whatever is available. There may be old building accounts, plans, maps, court records, charters, rental agreements and tax returns. Any of these may provide useful clues.

The archaeologist can, in turn, correct the picture of the past presented by written records and bring it to life. In England, for example, there have been interesting excavations at York and Winchester. In these and other digs, many new discoveries have added to the information provided by the records of the city, the charters, bills of sale, church records, old maps and the inscriptions on tombs. At Winchester, archaeologists were able to show the surprising fact that the grid pattern of the town streets belonged to a later period than they had previously supposed. It was of Anglo-Saxon and not Roman origin. Such excavations have revealed ordinary details of everyday life which were not

One of the pillars erected by King Aśoka.

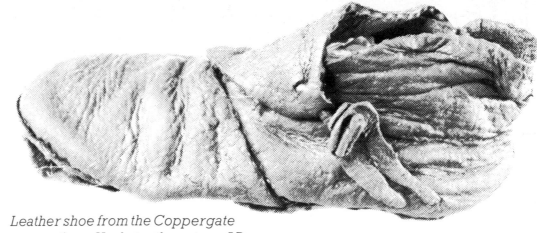

Leather shoe from the Coppergate excavations, York, tenth century AD.

A badge worn by a Roman slave: the inscription is a warrant for the slave's arrest if he ran away.

On this street plan of medieval Winchester, the Roman streets, which have almost disappeared, are shown in black, and the Anglo-Saxon streets are in blue.

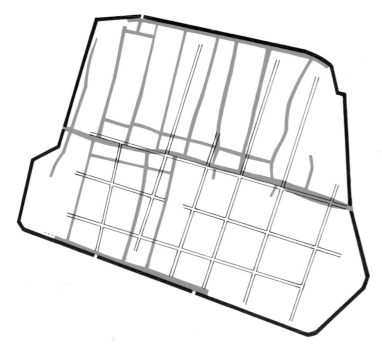

thought important enough to be included in written documents. The design and working methods of small shops and workshops have been investigated. At Coppergate in York, a complete Viking leather-working shop has been preserved in waterlogged soil. Equipment for curing, stretching and cutting leather has been found together with many half-completed shoes and purses.

Historical archaeology is not confined to Europe. Excavations in Australia have told us much about life in the early settlements. They have provided the sort of information which would never have been written down about contact between aborigines and white settlers. Most people only record unusual events. Excavations at Fort Toulouse in Alabama have produced many examples of the trade goods brought by the French colonizers in the eighteenth century. These give us a lot of information about what types of guns were being used and what kind of alcohol was supplied to the Cree Indian nation. Broken gin bottles, bits and pieces of gunlock plates, bullet moulds and gun flints are all that now remain.

Outstanding work has been carried out at Williamsburg, Jamestown and Yorktown on the east coast of the USA. Here the records of early colonial settlements have been used as a basis for large-scale excavations and reconstructions. Visitors to Williamsburg, capital of Virginia from 1699 to 1779, may catch a glimpse of everyday life in eighteenth century America. They can walk through the old town and its gardens, both accurately restored, and see the local inhabitants dressed in the costumes of the period. None of this would have been possible if historians and archaeologists had not worked together to re-create a bygone age.

Economic Archaeology

The first archaeologists concentrated upon finding and studying objects such as pots, brooches and tools made by prehistoric peoples. They took these artefacts as their foundation, and worked out systems to explain the development of ancient societies, purely through the things they left behind. These systems were based on the three principal materials used to make tools and weapons. Archaeologists still talk about the Stone, Bronze and Iron Ages. But today we are far more interested in *how* prehistoric groups lived, and ask many questions undreamt of by our predecessors. In the 1930s, a few archaeologists began to turn their attention away from artefacts and concentrate on how early groups related to and were affected by their geographical environment.

One of the first excavations to use this approach was that at Star Carr, Yorkshire. This Mesolithic (Middle Stone Age, 10 000–5000 BC) site was chosen because it was thought to contain well-preserved organic remains. These would help archaeologists to reconstruct the economy of the people who had lived there nine thousand years ago. A team of geologists, botanists and zoologists worked together with archaeologists in order to extract every possible scrap of evidence from the excavation.

The site at Star Carr produced many stone and bone tools and showed that the inhabitants had worked antlers to make hunting and fishing gear, such as netting needles, fish hooks and spearheads. The remains of a wooden paddle were found, indicating that they built small boats to use on the nearby lake. Thousands of finds of animal bones, plant remains and pollen grains were carefully studied in laboratories. By fitting together all the different pieces of information, it was possible to say that the site was occupied from late autumn to early spring by about twenty-five people. They came back to Star Carr every year for about twenty years, and lived on a log platform which they built on the edge of the lake.

Detailed information has been gathered about hunting peoples of the last century, such as some tribes of North American Indians. This has helped archaeologists to guess much about the Star Carr people. They probably ranged over about 500 square kilometres of territory containing about 3400 red deer. This was a plentiful supply of meat for the four or five family groups that lived there. Some of the deer stag skulls found in the excavations had been made into head dresses. These might have been used by hunters stalking game or worn for ceremonial dances.

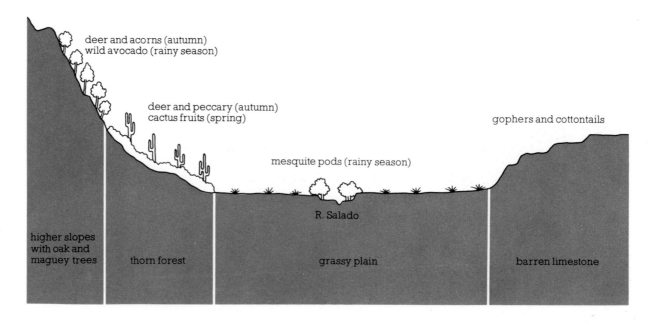

This section through the Tehuacán Valley, Mexico, shows wild food resources, and is an important stage in site catchment analysis.

deer and acorns (autumn)
wild avocado (rainy season)

deer and peccary (autumn)
cactus fruits (spring)

gophers and cottontails

mesquite pods (rainy season)

R. Salado

higher slopes with oak and maguey trees

thorn forest

grassy plain

barren limestone

Mask made from the front part of a deer skull with the antlers left in place, Star Carr, Yorkshire, about 7500 BC.

At Grimes Graves in Norfolk, Neolithic miners dug deep shafts to reach high quality layers of flint. These mines help archaeologists to understand the economy of this Neolithic society.

The greatest needs of both people and animals are to find food and to reproduce themselves. Human societies and ways of life have been greatly affected by their geographical environments. On the other hand, many peoples have tried to improve their surroundings by drainage or irrigation schemes, and so themselves have moulded their own environment. The archaeologists studying the pattern of human settlement in an area try to discover what supplies of raw material and foodstuffs were within reasonable reach of the village or cave being investigated. They often begin the study of an area by walking over every part of the landscape surrounding the main settlement site. They note all the different types of landform, soil, vegetation and animal life. They also locate water supplies, rock and mineral outcrops, and cave and rock shelters. This kind of study is known as site catchment analysis. Using this method, the pattern of human settlement was traced in the Virú valley of north Peru from five thousand years ago to the present day.

Archaeology Underwater

It was a terrible disaster when, in 1628, the great vessel Vasa sank suddenly in Stockholm harbour as she set out on her maiden voyage. For the archaeologist, however, it has meant a wonderful insight into life aboard a ship of that period. In 1961, after great effort, the vessel was raised again to the surface. The cabins and hold had filled with mud which had preserved many of the contents. Skeletons were found, fully clothed, their purses full of coins. The structure of the ship provided valuable evidence of seventeenth century methods of ship building, which would otherwise have been lost forever.

Underwater archaeology is a new subject. Like all archaeology, it must be very carefully recorded. Until recently this was almost impossible, as archaeologists could hardly venture beneath the water. Clumsy early diving suits needed air pumped from the surface. A very simple form of underwater excavation took place in 1904, when offerings to a rain god were dredged up from a sacred Maya pool at Chichén Itzá in Mexico. There were treasures of jade and gold as well as the bones of young people who had been sacrificed. However, it was not until 1942 that the aqualung was invented and archaeologists could suddenly penetrate depths they had not dreamt of and move about with ease.

Material comes to be under water in many ways. Parts of the Mediterranean sea routes are littered with shipwrecks of many periods. Sometimes earthquakes and landslips, like the one which destroyed Port Royal, Jamaica in 1692, cause important sites to sink under water. In other areas rising sea levels or sinking land, or the creation of new artificial lakes submerge sites. Some items are thrown into the water as offerings. The famous Iron Age Battersea shield may have found its way into the River Thames as an offering to a water god.

Each type of underwater deposit presents its own problems. When wrecks break up, their cargo and structure may be spread over a wide area, continually worn away and shifted by tides and storms. In warm climates they may become covered with corals and other marine growths.

A specially trained archaeologist wearing an aqualung investigates a shipwreck in tropical waters off Singapore.

In some regions heavy objects sink deep into silt which both preserves and hides them.

The methods used for excavation on land are specially adapted for underwater excavation. The archaeologist usually lays out a horizontal reference grid of wires or metal rods and measures vertical positions with surveying instruments.

It is difficult to excavate underwater. Disturbed deposits cloud the water and quickly settle back again. Mud or sand and small finds can often be removed by using an air hose.

The raising of the Vasa in Stockholm harbour. She was later restored.

The Battersea shield, made of bronze with enamel decoration, is a superb example of British craftsmanship at the time of the Roman conquest in AD 43.

Air is pumped down the outer sleeve of a long tube and bubbles back to the surface up the centre, taking with it the mud and objects. Large objects may be raised by attaching them to bags or balloons, which are then filled with air so they float up to the surface.

Not all underwater archaeology involves diving. When five Viking vessels were discovered in Roskilde Fjord, Norway, a special sort of walled dam was built around them. Then the water in which they lay was pumped away so they could be recorded and recovered.

Underwater archaeology often involves piecing together scattered and damaged fragments. At times it is the vessel itself, at others, its cargo. An unusual attempt to rescue a cargo began off the Scilly Islands a few years ago. Divers worked on the sailing ship Colossus, wrecked in 1798 while carrying to England hundreds of ancient Greek vases for the private collection of an English nobleman. Material once excavated on land was now being re-excavated underwater. Many fragments of this great collection have now been recovered and are slowly being pieced together.

The methods used in underwater archaeology are still being developed. The evidence lying submerged fills many gaps in the story told by dry-land archaeology.

Industrial Archaeology

Until the Industrial Revolution of the eighteenth and nine-teenth centuries, most goods were produced directly by human or animal energy. Then the steam engine was invented. Other sources of power were developed that speeded up production. Soon great quantities of standardized goods, made by machines, were flooding out from the factories of Europe and America. Vast new industrial cities sprang up almost overnight, near to essential iron, water and coal resources. These attracted workers who had previously lived in farming communities. As mass-production increased, new natural resources were discovered and developed. Communication between peoples and countries grew rapidly. Soon almost all parts of the world became linked in a vast trading network. The rate of change accelerated and the gap between industrialized societies and those that were not grew wider.

Industrial archaeologists study the early history of our modern machine-based society. This is a vast subject. It includes the study of factories, the machines themselves and the goods they produced. It also covers everything connected with this, such as the houses specially built for factory workers and the water supplies both they and the factories needed. The docks, railways, canals and locks used in carrying raw materials and finished products are also important, as are the warehouses, mining and smelting equipment, and even the clothing used by workers and the toys or ornaments they made from scrap. The archaeologist working in this field must have a firm understanding of the principles of engineering and, in some cases, of chemistry, mining geology and other subjects connected with industry.

Industrial archaeology is centred in northwestern Europe and North America. Here early inventions were produced and used in the eighteenth and nineteenth centuries. The spinning jenny revolutionized cotton spinning in Lancashire. Railways spread across the United States, linking east and west, only a few decades after pioneers had travelled the same ground in covered wagons.

The industrial archaeologist has several tasks. The first is to discover and record as much as possible about how things were produced. Working closely with historians, the archaeologist can use contemporary accounts of factories or railways, and may even succeed in finding original blueprints, patent drawings, or a firm's own records.

Steam locomotive, USA, 1870.

Canals (far left) revolutionized the transport of raw materials and finished goods from ports and factories.

The world's first iron bridge, built at Ironbridge, Shropshire, 1779.

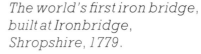

A medieval tile kiln.

Nevertheless, many questions can only be answered by fieldwork. Sometimes no excavation is needed. The steam engine, factory, crane or pump which interests the archaeologist may still be standing, even if in a neglected state. Here the task is to study and record, using photography to produce technical drawings. At other times it is necessary to dig. For example, at Saugus in Massachusetts, archaeologists excavated the seventeenth century village ironworks and smithy. Not only buildings were revealed but also details such as what fuel was used and how waste was dumped.

Industrial science moves forward quickly. Equipment is often destroyed once it has been replaced by more efficient machinery. Factory buildings are knocked down to make way for bigger ones. Canals are allowed to silt up and old machines are smashed for scrap. The industrial archaeologist must find and preserve these valuable examples of industrial history. Sometimes this requires a great deal of effort. The world's first iron-hulled steamship, the SS *Great Britain*, was recently rescued from a beach in the Falkland Islands where she had been rusting for many years. She was towed back to England to be restored and used as a floating museum.

One of the best ways of interesting the public and getting support for industrial archaeology is to restore machinery to working order and allow visitors to see it in action. Steam engines, pumping stations, early cars, trams, trains and aircraft all attract visitors. They become aware of the value in finding and preserving other examples before they are lost forever to future generations.

Rescue Archaeology

In the last two centuries we have become more and more aware of our past. We have developed better and better ways to recover knowledge of it. At the same time, however, we have created new and more efficient ways to destroy it. This has led to the development of rescue archaeology, which sets out to salvage archaeological evidence threatened by immediate destruction.

The Industrial Revolution triggered off great social, political and technical change in Europe and North America. In the present century this has spread over most of the world. We can alter the face of large areas of our planet in a way which would have been impossible only twenty or thirty years ago. This has led to a vast destruction of archaeological sites.

The range of this threat is enormous. New dams, new roads, large-scale mining, the expansion of cities and towns, and the bringing of virgin land under the plough change the natural environment. The uppermost layers of soil are moved and covered and it is just there that most archaeological remains are to be found. In some cases, such as the building of the Aswan Dam in Egypt, or the creation of the world's largest artificial lake behind the Volta Dam in Ghana, vast areas of land are submerged forever. These contain not only present-day towns and villages, but also the remains of many earlier ones. In other cases new buildings in ancient settlements, such as London or Athens, may need to have deep foundations which cut directly through important archaeological remains. Every time a pipe-line is laid or a road built evidence of the past is wiped out.

Rescue archaeology has developed to save as much of the past as possible in these circumstances. One of the aims of rescue archaeology is to make people aware of the dangers to their cultural heritage which exist today. In Britain, the USA, and many other countries, this is done by setting up local archaeological organizations and by encouraging young people to become interested in archaeology. These amateur archaeologists can then keep alert to any threats to archaeological sites and campaign to preserve them. Many countries have now passed laws to protect major archaeological remains from destruction.

The organizations must be provided with money to carry out excavations quickly and efficiently, before a site is bulldozed, drowned or buried forever. This may involve a major international operation such as that mounted at the temple of Abu Simbel in Egypt. There, buildings were taken to pieces and reconstructed above the new water level of the Aswan Dam. Or it may mean simply providing a few skilled professional archaeologists to direct a larger group of volunteer amateurs to survey and, if necessary, excavate sites under immediate threat. Also excavated material has to be properly stored, studied and published. In some cases, the companies and authorities actually involved in developing these sites have been persuaded to exhibit material. In this way, local people have been made aware of the importance of archaeology.

Rescue archaeology very often means emergency excavation which is forced upon archaeologists. Some archaeologists would prefer to excavate only those sites which they believe will test their theories and help solve particular problems. They dislike having to dig simply because a site is soon to be obliterated. Sometimes there is only time to dig a portion of a site rather than recover everything. Nevertheless, if rescue excavations are not carried out, unique evidence will be lost, and this evidence may, one day, be of great importance.

The lake created by the Aswan Dam in Egypt threatened to submerge the famous temple of Abu Simbel, built by order of Pharaoh Ramses II between 1290 and 1223 BC. Engineers cut the huge sandstone temple into more than 1000 blocks which were then rebuilt on a higher site nearby.

Experiments in Archaeology

Archaeologists use experiments to check the conclusions they have reached from the evidence of their excavations. They also try to solve the problems that arise when the buried material they find has not been completely preserved. This is not a new idea, for in the last century scholars experimented with making flint tools, General Pitt-Rivers studied the ways ditches silted up, and in 1893 an exact copy of a Viking ship was test-sailed across the Atlantic. Since those days, many archaeologists have tried to reproduce methods of doing things which have been revealed by excavations. They have also tried to find out how objects might have been made and used. Today these experiments are more frequent than ever before. They are carried out on a large scale with great attention to detail.

Many experimental reconstructions have centred on food production. In both Scandinavia and Britain, experimental farms have been set up where archaeologists have used and recorded the effects of, for example, slash and burn agriculture. Early farmers cut down trees and shrubs to clear a plot in the forest. They burned the vegetation and the ashes fertilized the soil. After several crops had been harvested, the soil became exhausted and yields became smaller. Then a new clearing was made and cultivated while the old one was allowed to grow back into the forest.

The experiments were interesting because they showed exactly how the pollen remains changed when this kind of agriculture was practised. If pollen analysis from an excavation reveals a pattern which matches that of pollen from these experiments, archaeologists can be certain that the prehistoric farmers they are studying were using slash and burn methods.

Archaeologists have experimented with early types of plough drawn by oxen to see how efficient they were in breaking the ground. They also worked out how long it

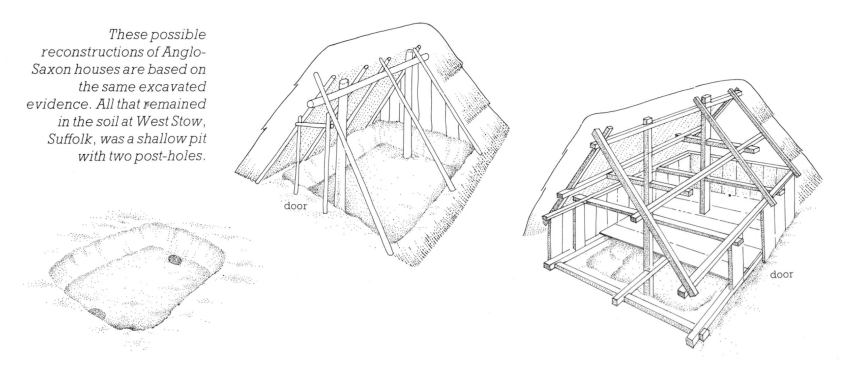

These possible reconstructions of Anglo-Saxon houses are based on the same excavated evidence. All that remained in the soil at West Stow, Suffolk, was a shallow pit with two post-holes.

door

door

Iron Age cattle are used in a ploughing experiment at Butser Hill Farm Project, Hampshire.

took a farmer to plough his fields. Iron Age cattle have been created by breeding back from modern strains. They have also been butchered in the ways which are suggested by bones found in archaeological sites. This showed how much meat was on the most popular joints and how many people they may have fed.

Experiments have been made into how food was stored. In Guatemala, tests on bottle-shaped pits lined with plaster have shown that they were used for water storage. A series of experiments showed that similar pits found in other parts of Central America were useless for water storage but excellent for the dry storage of the ramon nut. This was a very important source of food to the ancient Maya.

One kind of experimental reconstruction involves trying to build houses which would fit in with the pattern of ancient remains, for example postholes or stone foundations discovered by excavation. In several cases, these experiments have helped to show that earlier ideas on how they were built were wrong. The types of roof or heights of wall that archaeologists had visualized would never have stayed up.

Experiments studying natural forces, such as erosion, which work on archaeological remains, may be said to go back to Charles Darwin. He studied how the activities of earthworms buried objects left on the surface of the ground. Worms take discarded soil to the surface and leave it there in casts. Modern archaeologists have built different types of earthwork and then observed how they settle, wear away, silt up and are recolonized by plants. From this kind of experiment, they can work out how long earthwork fortifications were in use and how high the original earthbanks were. Attempts have been made to reproduce the conditions under which the stone in the walls of Scottish Iron Age forts became heated to temperatures so high that the rocks melted and fused together. The fires that caused this may have been lit by the builders to produce particularly strong defensive walls.

The variety of present-day archaeological experiments is enormous. They range from navigating outrigger vessels on the Pacific Ocean, to testing how efficient Bronze Age metal or leather shields were against swords and arrows. The leather shields proved the most efficient when the leather had been hardened in hot water and beaten into shape. The bronze ones were probably ornamental. Experiments are valuable because they reveal any shaky conclusions that have been reached by excavation. Sometimes they provide revolutionary information. But normally the archaeologist has only been able to make an informed guess at what happened on the site in ancient times.

The Origins of Mankind

For how long have human beings walked the Earth? When did they part company with their ape-like ancestors? What did they inherit from them? Archaeologists cannot yet have definite answers to these questions. However, in recent years they have made astonishing discoveries which suggest how they may eventually be answered.

Most of these discoveries have been made in East Africa, an area where early hominid fossil remains are preserved and easily reached. Many finds have been made by the Leakey family, Louis, his wife Mary and son Richard, excavating in the Olduvai Gorge in Tanzania and at other sites. To the north, in the Afar region of Ethiopia, American archaeologists have also added to our knowledge of our early ancestors.

The evidence is slender. For the first three million or so years of our history, we have only a few boxes of fragmentary fossilized bones and some shaped stones. Yet from these scraps of skull, hand bones, pelvises and other fragments, carefully cut or dissolved out of the surrounding rock, we can begin to sketch the outlines of our own past.

The picture to emerge so far is like this. Possibly as much as four million years ago, creatures who could walk upright and had comparatively large brains were living on the savanna, or vast grass-covered plains, of what is now Africa. This was far earlier than anyone had believed likely until very recently. These creatures seem to have evolved from a type of ape called *Ramapithecus*, which existed about twelve million years ago. The hominid line had by now branched off from the main ape line. There seem to have been at least three distinct types of early hominid. Two of these, called *Australopithecus*, eventually disappeared. The third, *Homo habilis* ('handy Man'), is thought to be one of our ancestors.

But when can we say 'This is a human being'? Walking upright was an important stage in our evolution. It meant that the hands became free to carry, use and eventually make things. A large brain was further evidence of development. But most significant were the signs that hominids were able to make things, shown at first by simple tools. These tools were roughly modified pebbles and stones. They have been found at Olduvai in association with hominid remains about one to two million years old. It is thought that *Homo habilis* made and used these.

As tool using continued, slowly becoming more sophisticated, other signs appeared which set our early ancestors apart from animals. Traces of fire, dating back to about

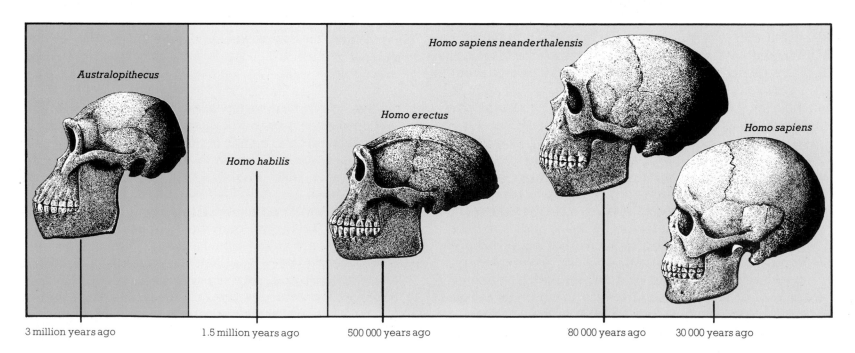

Australopithecus

Homo habilis

Homo erectus

Homo sapiens neanderthalensis

Homo sapiens

3 million years ago   1.5 million years ago   500 000 years ago   80 000 years ago   30 000 years ago

This skull of Peking Man, from Chou K'ou Tien, China, is about half a million years old.

Near Lake Eyasi, Tanzania, the footprints of early humans have been found. Two individuals, possibly a male and a female, walked across soft lakeside mud which became fossilized. Their footprints have given precious information about the development of Mankind's upright posture.

two and a half million years ago, have been found at Lake Turkana in East Africa, possibly used, though probably not made by early hominids. What is thought to be the earliest discovered human building was also found in East Africa. This is a two million year old circle of stones. Some of the stones were placed on top of others and these may have anchored the edges of a shelter made of branches.

About half a million years ago in Africa a new form of tool began to appear which had many uses. It was the teardrop shaped handaxe. This was probably invented by the gradually developing group of our ancestors known as *Homo erectus* ('upright Man') which was soon to spread from Africa into other areas of the world. By about half a million years ago, it is clear that fire was under human con-trol. The pace of human development began to accelerate. Peking Man, the name given to *Homo erectus* in China, may have practised cannibalism. This is shown by the way human skulls were broken to extract the brains inside. Evidence from Spain indicates large group elephant hunts 300 000 years ago. By 50 000 years ago, Neanderthalers, possibly our most recent ancestors, carefully buried their dead and covered the bodies with flowers, as at Shanidar in Iraq.

There is still so much we do not know. We do not know when early people first began to speak or when they developed religious beliefs. Nevertheless, we can now see that our origins go back much further than we ever thought possible.

The First Toolmakers

*Front and side views of a chopper tool
(below), an early handaxe (centre) and
a later, more carefully made,
tear-drop shaped handaxe (right)*

  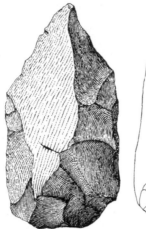  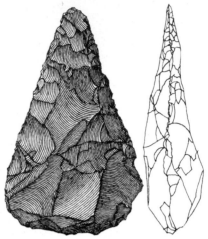

*Wooden spear-tip from Clacton-on-Sea,
Essex, 300 000 to 250 000 years old.*

It used to be common to define the human species as the only animal that used tools. We now know that chimpanzees in their natural surroundings will poke sticks into termite mounds to get insects for eating. Earlier writers had pointed out that the Californian sea otter used stones to smash mollusc shells balanced on its chest as it floated on its back. Nevertheless, tool using still remains a standard by which to judge Mankind. We belong to the only species which deliberately creates tools to a set pattern, rather than simply adapting natural objects. No other species uses tools to make other tools. We have now reached the point where we have machines to control machines which produce other machines for us! No other species is dependent on making and using tools for its survival.

The earliest implements which can be identified as tools come from East Africa, with some of the earliest hominid fossils. In the 1930s Louis Leakey found roughly chipped pebbles which he called chopper tools. He argued that these were the types of tools used before the well known

stone handaxes came into existence. In the early 1950s he found similar chopper tools in the lowest and earliest bed at Olduvai, and called the type Oldowan. In the 1960s new dating techniques, mainly the potassium-argon method, indicated that such tools were about two million years old. They were far older than anyone had considered possible. More recently, quartz tools have been found in the Omo valley, Ethiopia, which also have an age of two million years. Nobody knows for certain which early hominid group produced these. Many archaeologists favour *Homo habilis* as the tool-user.

Nineteenth century archaeologists thought that the earliest tools would be crude in form. Many collections were made of eoliths, or 'dawn stones', from the Pliocene period (five million years ago) and Miocene period (twenty-five million years ago). It was difficult to be sure if early people had fashioned these ancient stone tools. Natural crushing, sharp changes of temperature and many other non-human forces can produce pebbles and rocks which look very similar to early chipped stone tools. For a tool

A modern flint working experiment in Denmark.

to be accepted as an artefact, it must come from a period and a place which are recognized and dated. It must be one of a series of stones showing the same broad pattern of alteration. The many collections of eoliths are not now thought to be genuine. Leakey's Oldowan collection, however, was quite clearly made up of tools rather than of products of natural action. The fact that they existed alongside the remains of extinct hominids raised the whole question of how and when human beings parted company from their early ape-like ancestors.

Primitive people may have scavenged the prey of wild animals. Once they began to kill large beasts themselves they would need weapons. The earliest wooden spear so far discovered dates only from about 300 000 to 250 000 years ago, but it is possible that spears were in use far earlier. Early hunters would also need tools to cut up their kill, so hunting and tool using must have gone together. Maybe the need to work together when hunting fostered the development of language. The hunters needed to explain ideas about past hunting expeditions or future ones.

This would encourage them to talk about things outside their immediate surroundings.

The chopper-tools of the earliest period are succeeded, after a million years or more, by a widespread use of the handaxe. This seems to be the work of *Homo erectus*. We are still not certain how these handaxes were used. They were probably multi-purpose tools. Certainly, they were used in hunting and cutting up game. This is proved by finds of handaxes alongside the carcasses of large game animals. Most handaxes are core tools which were chipped from a lump of stone. During the million year period in which they were made, their style and the way they were made became more and more sophisticated. There is evidence of an increasing number of specialized tools made during the later part of the Old Stone Age (30 000–10 000 BC). By this time, the great variety of 'tool-kits' shows how traditional methods of making tools were being adapted to suit the local conditions and local types of game. This is evidence that people were beginning to control their environment.

Hunters and Gatherers

Men have hunted and women have gathered for nearly all of their time on Earth. Agriculture and animal herding have developed only recently in our history. Even today, several groups still live in the ancient way, though they are confined to remote areas which are useless to farming or herding peoples. A hundred years ago there were many more of these hunters. Now they are nearly all extinct. Much of archaeology is the story of man the hunter and, usually, woman the gatherer.

Our hominid ancestors probably lived on a mixed diet of vegetable matter and any insects and small creatures they could catch. Even today grubs and termites are favourite foods in many tropical areas. The need to co-operate in hunting larger animals may have pushed our early ancestors forward along the evolutionary path. They developed tools to kill and cut up large beasts. They needed to work together in groups and so speech developed and their mental ability increased. Peking Man, who lived about 750 000 years ago, was clearly a great hunter. The remains of many species of animal have been found at the Chinese site of Chou K'ou Tien. Deer, leopard, cave-bear, sabre-tooth tiger, hyena, elephant, horse and boar were hunted. From the Mesolithic period we have the remains of fish nets and traps. Domestic rubbish heaps, called shell middens, have been found in coastal areas. These tell us that some early groups relied on fish and shellfish for food and camped near their food supplies.

Most hunting and gathering peoples have definite patterns in their lives. They tend to divide the work between the men, who concentrate on catching and killing the larger animals, and the women, children and the elderly, who gather roots, berries, fruits and insects. Life also has a definite seasonal pattern. During part of the year, animal and plantfood is abundant and large groups of people can gather together to hunt and feast. At other times, game is scarce and the people must split into small groups and spread out, following the game as it searches for food.

The archaeologist comes across several distinct sorts of site. There are those occupied by a few people during the season when game was scarce, and those occupied by larger groups when food was plentiful. There are also kill sites which are places at which animals were killed. The first two kinds might be occupied year after year, and kill sites may be close to both sorts of camp. By examining the settlement sites, archaeologists can reconstruct the size of the group present and discover details of their diet. By studying the plant and pollen evidence, they may also work out at which season the site was used. At the famous Mesolithic site at Star Carr in Yorkshire, the organic remains showed that red deer was the preferred game, but aurochs (an extinct type of wild ox), elks and water birds were also hunted. By studying all the various sites, it may be possible to work out precisely over which territory the hunting groups ranged.

A great deal can be learned from kill sites. They not only give evidence of hunting methods, but the animal skeletons may also contain broken or unrecovered weapons. The way the animals were butchered may tell us something about the size of the hunting band. At the Olsen–Chubbuck site in a dry ravine in Colorado, the remains of nearly two hundred bison have been excavated. They were slaughtered in about 6500 BC. The bones

Careful excavation of bison skeletons at the Olsen-Chubbuck site, Colorado, led to the discovery of the way in which Indian hunters butchered the animals 8500 years ago.

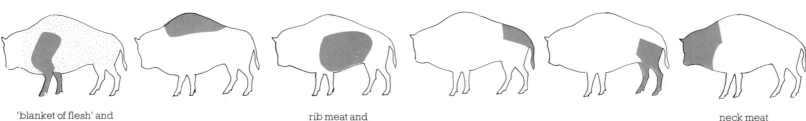

'blanket of flesh' and front legs   hump meat   rib meat and inner organs   pelvic girdle   hind legs   neck meat and tongue

A cave-painting of an Old Stone Age hunter attacked by a bison, Lascaux, France.

Women of the Chenchu tribe, India, digging up edible roots.

lay in three distinct layers. The whole corpses were at the bottom, slightly cut about ones in the middle and then, at the top, the skeletons which had been dismembered. The bison had been stampeded into the ravine from the north. The first to fall in were trapped by those which crashed on top of them. The way the bones of the dismembered skeletons were piled indicated the order in which the topmost carcasses had been cut up. Judging from the work involved, the amount of meat produced and how long it would probably stay fresh, it was calculated that the group of hunters and their dependants consisted of about a hundred and fifty people. The remains of newborn calves were also found, which showed that the hunt had taken place in May or early June.

The First Farmers

In many parts of the world, people lived by hunting and gathering until very recently. Where game and wild plants suitable for food were plentiful, they were able to develop large permanent settlements like Lepenski Vir in Yugoslavia. Here the population relied heavily on fishing in the Danube. Villages and towns did not develop in most parts of the world until our ancestors changed from hunting and gathering to growing crops and tending animals. They became farmers.

Archaeologists once thought that this change to agriculture happened fairly suddenly. It led to a rapid increase in food production, population and the growth of villages. This was known as the Neolithic Revolution. But there are now good reasons for believing that it was a slower, more subtle series of events which occurred at different times and in different parts of the world. It happened at different speeds in different regions. Farmers were growing wheat and barley about nine thousand years ago in the Zagros and Taurus Mountains of Mesopotamia and Anatolia

(Turkey). But it was not until about four thousand years later that Scandinavian peoples first started growing crops.

Hunters and gatherers did not usually kill the wild animals and uproot the plants on which they depended in an uncontrolled way. They tended to concentrate on particular types and ages of animals or particular plant foods. Rarely did they threaten to wipe out the species. Some gatherers changed their surroundings by burning or clearing undergrowth, to help favourite kinds of plants to grow. Others lived in close, almost mutual, dependence with wild animals such as reindeer. As early farmers gradually bred wild plants and animals, the species changed irreversibly. The main cause of this was the way they brought about genetic changes in the animals and plants to suit their own needs. In this way they made those species dependent on them forever. Domesticated animals were separated from the wild animals to avoid interbreeding. Plants were grown in places where particular

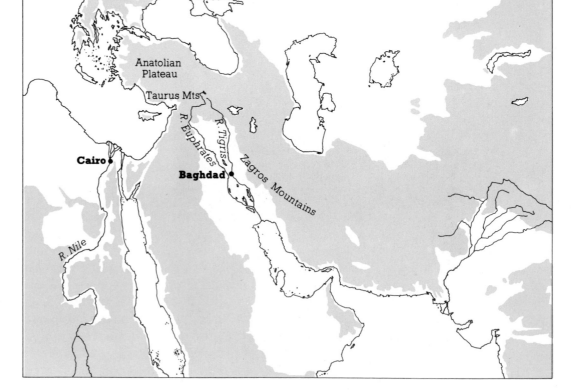

This map shows the areas of early agriculture in the Near East. Surprisingly, they are all in dry areas where food plants did not grow in abundance naturally. People living under these hard conditions had to develop methods to guarantee their food supply, and so plant cultivation and animal domestication began.

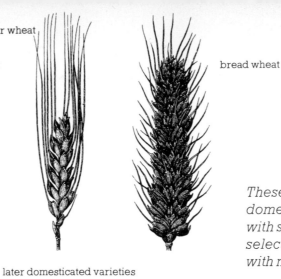

emmer wheat

einkorn wheat

bread wheat

wild wheat   early cultivated wheat   later domesticated varieties

These drawings show stages in the domestication of wheat. Wild types with small seeds were gradually selectively bred to produce varieties with much bigger grains.

varieties could thrive and crossbreed. In this way strains were produced which would ripen within a short period. They were convenient for people to harvest and would not easily seed themselves. The bond between early farmers and their animals became stronger as they came to rely on draught animals to pull their ploughs and carts and on the milk and wool from goats and sheep.

Wall painting of farming on the estate of an ancient Egyptian, Nakht, from his tomb at Thebes, about 1500 BC.

The first steps in cultivating plants seem to have been taken in areas which were on the borders of, and not in, the fertile alluvial valleys of the Tigris and Euphrates rivers of Mesopotamia. Archaeologists once thought that the lowlands of Mesopotamia were the birthplace of the Neolithic Revolution. But it has been shown that the Zagros and Taurus Mountains, the basins of the Anatolian Plateau and the high, arid basin around the Tehuacán valley, Mexico, contain sites with evidence of the earliest cultivation of cereals. The conditions here were very difficult and early settlers probably had to take deliberate steps to develop and foster local food supplies.

If we study how modern crops originated and developed, and where the related wild species occur, we can work out where they may first have been cultivated. It is far more difficult to interpret animal bones to tell if they are from wild or domesticated species. But the proportion of certain ages or sexes of animals in the archaeological record may show that early farmers had started to breed and maintain the type of herd they preferred.

Agriculture was well under way by 5000 BC in many areas scattered throughout Anatolia and Mesopotamia. At the same period, people living in settlements in these areas had domesticated animals such as dogs, goats, sheep and possibly cattle. In Mexico, maize cultivation began at about the same period, but it took a longer time before cultivated plants were more important in the diet than gathered food. The breeding of plants, such as rice, yam and sweet potato, happened independently in other areas such as China, western Asia and Africa. Agriculture was being practised as early as 5000 BC in the highlands of New Guinea, where taro, a starchy root, was being grown in specially drained and fertilized plots.

The Origins of Cities

The first cities grew up about 5500 years ago. They had fairly small populations and served as administrative, trading and religious centres which were in direct contact with the surrounding farmland. City life, as we know it, only began 100–150 years ago, during the Industrial Revolution, when people migrated from the countryside to the new industrial and manufacturing centres.

The world's earliest cities grew from villages in Mesopotamia and in the Nile valley of Egypt about 3500–3000 BC. Soon afterwards, cities appeared in the Indus valley of Pakistan and in China along the Yellow River. These cities developed because of the annual flooding of the great rivers, which fertilized the land and made it possible to grow large crops of grain every year. Much later, in the fourth century AD, cities were built in Central America. Similar conditions seem to have encouraged these centres of great civilizations to grow. Farming methods had to be efficient so that a surplus of food, usually grain which is easy to store, could be built up to feed larger numbers of

people. When this happened not everyone needed to work on the land. Some people began to specialize in crafts such as pottery and jewellery making. Many early civilizations used bronze tools, ploughed their fields and used the wheel in transport and machinery. All the early civilizations were literate. Writing is an important part of city life. Accounts and inventories can be kept, laws and religious teachings written down.

As the work load was shared out and some people learned to write, a ruling class developed. This group usually controlled both civil government and religious power. This aristocracy, once established, could organize the huge teams of labourers needed in large scale construction work, such as building fortifications, irrigation systems, temples and palaces.

The great Indus civilization, which flourished in India and Pakistan about 2300 to 1750 BC, dominated the plains of the Indus River and its tributaries. Wheat and barley were the main crops grown to feed the citizens of Harappa

This stern-faced stone statue of a priest-king was found in the citadel of Mohenjo-Daro.

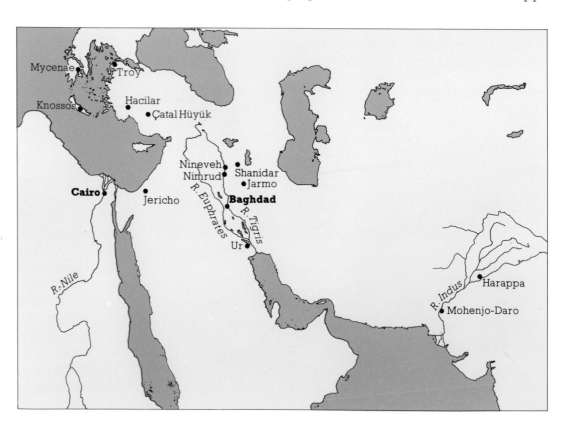

Early cities of the Near East.

The citadel, Mohenjo-Daro.

Mohenjo-Daro, excavations in the citadel revealed a large bath like a swimming-pool and a spacious assembly hall.

East of the citadel lay the residential part of the city. Houses, which varied in size from many-roomed mansions to one-roomed flats, were laid out in a grid-pattern. Homes were built of standard-sized mud bricks with wooden roofs and had blank windowless walls facing the main street. Entrances and windows were in side streets and courtyards. The paved streets were kept very clean. Nearly every house had a rubbish bin and a special bathroom which was linked to an elaborate drainage system.

The mysterious Indus script has still to be deciphered. Inscriptions in this language have been found on many seals and seal impressions. They were probably used to secure bales of merchandise and bore the name of the owner. Uniform weights and measures were in use; sets of weights have been found at Mohenjo-Daro. Long-distance trade between the cities of the Indus civilization and ancient Mesopotamia was well established. Trade contacts reached far to the east and west for precious stones, north to Afghanistan for silver and south to Mysore for gold. Within the Indus area bronze, iron and stone tools were designed to a regular pattern, and styles in pottery, jewellery and seal motifs are remarkably similar throughout the whole area.

and Mohenjo-Daro, the twin capital cities, about 640 kilometres apart. Life in these early cities was highly organized. The cities themselves were also carefully planned. The area was divided into an upper citadel and a lower residential area. The citadels were fortresses used for defensive and religious purposes. They also contained huge granaries complete with ventilation systems to prevent the stored grain from rotting. At Harappa, the ruined mud-brick walls, twelve metres thick, still stand to a height of fifteen metres, protecting the heart of the city. At

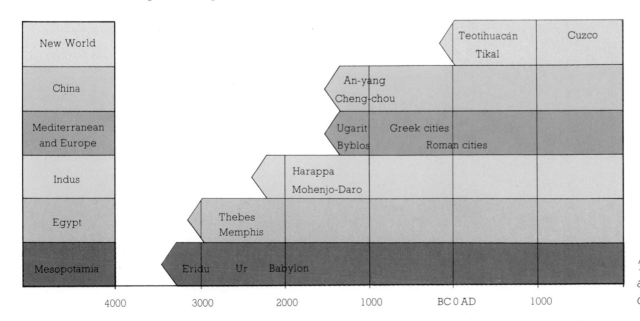

This time-chart shows where and when the world's great civilizations developed.

Writing and its Decoding

Writing was invented about 3500 BC in Mesopotamia. Before then pictures and signs were used to convey meaning. Now priests and kings had within their grasp the power to record speech. Writing began as drawings of the things referred to (pictograms). It soon developed to represent ideas (ideograms) and then, most important of all, the sounds of speech. The effects were profound. Until this point, knowledge could only be passed on by direct example and by word of mouth. Now it could be stored, accumulated and passed on to people many kilometres or generations apart.

Writing can therefore help us to understand the ideas and thoughts of people who died long before we were born. But first we must be able to read their writing. For many years, scholars have struggled to decipher the scripts of long dead civilizations and to release the knowledge locked in them.

To decipher an unknown script, we must first know or guess the language the writer was using. We must also obtain as many texts in that script and language as possible. We will then have a body of material to work on and to test our interpretations. Finally, we must link the signs and symbols used to sounds, words, phrases and meanings in that language and discover the language's grammar.

Reading an unknown language is much easier if the same text can be found written in a known language. It was just such a discovery which led to the decipherment of Egyptian hieroglyphics, the picture-like writing of the ancient Egyptian priests. In 1799 Napoleon's troops discovered, at Rosetta in Egypt, a stone on which there was an inscription in three scripts. One was Greek, the others ancient Egyptian scripts, hieroglyphic and a cursive, or flowing, form known as demotic. It was soon realized that the same passage might be written in each language.

An English scholar, Thomas Young, noted that some of the hieroglyphs enclosed in oval frames (cartouches) represented the name of the king, Ptolemy, in the readable Greek text. A young French scholar, Jean-François Champollion, worked on from there. He established that there were three times as many signs in the hieroglyphic text as in the Greek text. Each hieroglyph, therefore, could not represent a single word, for there would be more words in one text than the other. He then worked out the phonetic or sound value for the names in the cartouches, aided by his realization that the demotic and hieroglyphic scripts had both been used to write a language related to Coptic. This was the language of Christian Egyptians spoken about AD 500–700. This gave him many clues to the structure of words and their sounds, and soon he had cracked the code. In 1824 he published his findings. The way was clear for a greater understanding of ancient Egypt.

The decoding of ancient cuneiform inscriptions from Assyria was also helped by the discovery of the same text in different languages. There is a huge triple inscription

A clay tablet from Knossos, Crete, left, inscribed in Linear B, the earliest known form of written Greek, dated to about 1300 BC, and, below, the development of cuneiform symbols.

Pictograms			Sumerian		Babylonian	Assyrian	Meaning
3500 BC upright	3100 BC turned to left	2800 BC	2400 BC Linear	Cuneiform	1700 BC	700 BC	
							head/front
							bird

The name of the Egyptian pharaoh, Ptolemy, written in hieroglyphs and surrounded by an oval cartouche which gave magical protection. The same royal name was found on the Rosetta Stone.

The Rosetta Stone. The upper inscription is in hieroglyphic characters, the middle in demotic and the lower in Greek.

on the sheer face of a cliff in Iran, the Behistun Rock. The inscription was put there in 516 BC at the order of Darius I, King of Persia, to proclaim his victories. The text is in Elamite, Old Persian and Babylonian. Henry Rawlinson copied it in the 1830s and 1840s. He found a key to help unlock the code in the favourite Persian royal title of 'King of Kings'. There was a recurring phrase in the inscription which seemed to fit this. Gradually, he was able to read and translate the Old Persian text and then the other texts.

The most famous decipherment of recent years is that of Linear B. This is a pictographic script, first found in 1900 on clay tablets from Knossos in Crete and dating from the thirteenth century BC. In 1952 Michael Ventris, a war-time code-breaker and amateur archaeologist, discovered that the language used was an early form of Greek. The inscribed clay tablets finally proved to be mainly stock-taking lists and inventories!

There are still scripts that await decipherment, such as Linear A from Crete and the writings of the Indus Valley civilization. However, it may be a computer not an unaided human brain that will unlock these doors to the past.

Pottery and the Wheel

Pottery making and the discovery of the wheel are among the most important human inventions. They are vitally linked, for the wheel, first used on vehicles, was later used in the making of pottery. It became the basis of the countless rotary machines, with parts turning on an axis, without which our present world could not exist.

The first baked clay objects so far discovered date from about 25 000 BC. Stone Age artists had discovered that figurines (small statuettes) modelled in easily worked clay would harden when placed near a fire. The first known pottery vessels come from Japan and date from around 10 000 BC. At Mureybet in Syria, porous pots were made in about 8000 BC. Early pottery is also known from about 7500 BC at Ganjdareh, Iran. Exactly where and when pottery was first invented has still to be discovered. But by 6000 BC there was widespread use of hand-made pottery in the Zagros region of Iraq. By 5000 BC specialist potters were beginning to appear.

The pottery of this early period shows great technical skill and is often beautifully decorated. Most of it was made by methods still in use in many parts of the world. It was built up by smoothing together long coils of clay, or pulled up from a large lump, or made by joining rolled out sheets of clay. By 5000 BC a two chambered kiln had been invented, which separated the pots from the fire that was to bake them. This was a great improvement on the bonfire where the pots were simply placed in a pit beneath an open fire. By 4000 BC pots were being spun on a slow, hand or foot turned, turntable. A thousand years later the fast wheel had been invented. This was a wheel, perhaps with a lower fly wheel, which was kept spinning, so that the speed at which the lump of clay turned helped to shape its form. It was very much like a modern potter's wheel. This led to pottery being made to a set pattern and being mass produced.

Pottery depends on the melting together of plate-like particles in clay to produce a hard substance. Much primitive pottery was fired at well below 1000°C and was not fused all the way through. The invention and spread of

Painted pot from the Nazca Valley, Peru, made between 200 BC and AD 600. The human figure is flanked by two trophy heads, and wears a tunic decorated with snarling animal heads.

The earliest pottery yet found, from Fukui, Japan, dated about 10 000 BC.

An Assyrian cylinder seal with a cuneiform inscription and a scene from a lion hunt. The huntsman stands in a light chariot with two spoked wheels.

The Royal Standard of Ur, dated at about 2750 BC, shows carts with solid wheels pulled into battle by teams of four asses.

pottery helped early people when they settled in one place and lived in villages. It allowed them to store liquids and grain and replace the earlier sorts of wooden, hide, basketry or gourd vessels. Pottery seems to have been developed at different times, in different parts of the world. The first American pottery is dated to about 3000 BC and pottery was in use in China by about 4500 BC.

In the West we associate the wheel with transport. As early as 3000 BC wheeled vehicles were in use in Sumeria (the earliest civilization in southern Mesopotamia) for overland transport. It is likely that wheels evolved from tree trunks used as rollers to shift heavy weights. Early wheeled vehicles seem to have developed after sledges, which were well suited to the sandy summers and muddy winters of Sumeria. The earliest wheels discovered were solid discs made of three pieces of wood. Examples of wagons using such wheels were excavated at Ur and date from

about 2700 BC. Remains of skeletons show that these were pulled by oxen. Sometime between 2000 and 1500 BC two revolutionary things happened. The spoked wheel was invented which was lighter and stronger but more difficult to make. Also horses began to be used to pull wheeled vehicles. For many hundreds of years after this the chariot was an important factor in warfare.

Although the history of the West is closely involved with the use of the wheel, it was not known or used until recently in many areas of the world. In America, although wheeled toys were made, everything that had to be moved was carried by humans or on pack animals. But after the horse was introduced by Europeans to North America, goods were dragged behind. In Africa, wheeled vehicles were used in the Sahara in about AD 300. However, their use died out and the wheel was not used in Africa south of the Sahara until European colonization.

The Copper Age

The use of metal, like the spread of farming and pottery, reached different parts of the world at different times. Copper was the first metal to be used for making tools after stone, though in the old Three Age System, the Bronze Age was supposed to follow on directly after the New Stone Age. The Copper Age, or Chalcolithic, is the name used for the period of European prehistory from 6000 to 2000 BC. It was a time when flaked and polished stone was still the normal material for tools, but copper was used to make ornamental objects and ceremonial weapons.

At the ancient town of Çatal Hüyük in Anatolia, nuggets of native copper were cold-hammered into shape to make beads for necklaces at about 6000 BC. Later it was discovered that native copper and copper ores could be melted and poured into moulds to make more complicated shapes. The smelting of ores and casting of metal (metallurgy) represent a great advance in prehistoric technology. Copper metallurgy was known in Mesopotamia from about 4000 BC, centuries before the first civilizations grew up. Copper smelting developed at Çatal Hüyük before 5000 BC. Archaeological finds of copper axes in southeastern Europe and large urban settlements such as Karanova in Bulgaria suggest that copper working was well-established in the Balkans by 4000 BC. Metal prospectors and traders explored the rich copper sources of the Carpathian and Slovakian mountains. They may have travelled to Iberia (modern Spain and Portugal) in search of new ore deposits.

The Beaker People of western Europe seem to be the latest group belonging to the Copper Age. Between 2300 BC and 1700 BC they migrated from Iberia eastwards as far as Poland and northwards to the British Isles. They introduced the use of copper into Britain and put pottery beakers in the graves of their dead. People often put grave goods, such as jewellery, food, drink, money and clothing, into graves to equip the dead person for the afterlife. The Beaker people buried beautifully made flint arrow heads and archers' wrist guards made of stone, gold earrings and copper pins and knives with their dead. In England, they were responsible for building the huge circular monument at Avebury. They also constructed the 'blue stone' circle at Stonehenge.

In the Americas, the earliest known metalwork in both continents belongs to the 'Old Copper' people. They

hearths	
mud and timber walls	
trench with palisade	
postholes	

Plan of the Copper Age village at Polyanista, Bulgaria, which existed about 4500 BC.

Rolled sockets and points from the Old Copper Culture, in the Great Lakes area of North America.

flourished from 4000 to 2000 BC in the area of the Great Lakes of Michigan, Wisconsin and Ontario. The Old Copper metalworkers never discovered how to smelt ores or cast molten copper. Instead they hammered out knives, chisels, axes, harpoon heads and projectile points from naturally occurring lumps of copper. These tools are copies of earlier models made in other materials such as stone, bone, wood and shell. The main advance in this age was the making of rolled points and sockets for spear-heads, which fixed them more securely onto their shafts.

Much later, in about AD 200, the coppersmiths of the Hopewell Culture, in Ohio, produced hammered-out copper sheet. They cut this to shape and decorated it with intricate designs pushed from the back so they stood out in relief. They made bird and snake effigies, rings, ear ornaments, breastplates and head-dresses, and even large axe blades. Most of what is known about the Hopewell people comes from grave goods found in large burial mounds. There are many exotic treasures such as conch shells from the Gulf of Mexico, obsidian blades from the Southwest or Rockies, canine teeth from grizzly bears, inlaid with river pearls, and mysterious hand shapes cut from sheets of mica brought from Virginia. The villages of this artistic people were built in the fertile valleys where they grew corn and hunted and gathered.

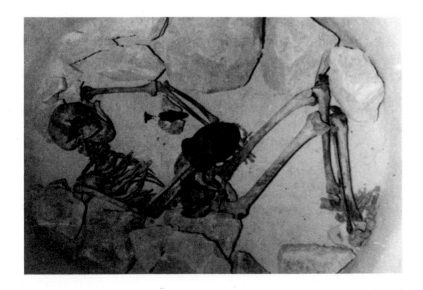

A Beaker burial from Shrewton, Wiltshire, complete with a typical Beaker pot and flaked flint knife.

The Bronze Age

Bronze is made by a deliberate mixture of the metals copper and tin. These produce a combination, or alloy, which is far more useful than either of its parts. Bronze is much tougher than copper and easier to cast. Edged tools and weapons stay sharper longer. A mixture of 10 per cent tin to 90 per cent copper was soon discovered to be the ideal alloy. However, early bronzesmiths often had to make do with far less tin. It is a rare mineral and difficult to extract using primitive mining and panning techniques.

The major sources of tin in prehistoric Europe were Cornwall, northwest Iberia and Bohemia. The biggest copper-bearing deposits were in central Europe. Mineral prospectors from the early states of Anatolia and Mesopotamia, which had been using bronze since about 4000 BC, travelled across Europe looking for ores. One of the most important results of the development of metal-using civilizations was that a trade in raw materials and finished objects was created. This produced a network of routes by sea, river and land. It also led to the development of a class of middlemen, local chiefs who gained control of and organized the supply and exchange of raw materials and exotic products. These middlemen became very

Bronze Age harp player from the Greek Island of Amorgos, dated 2400 to 2200 BC.

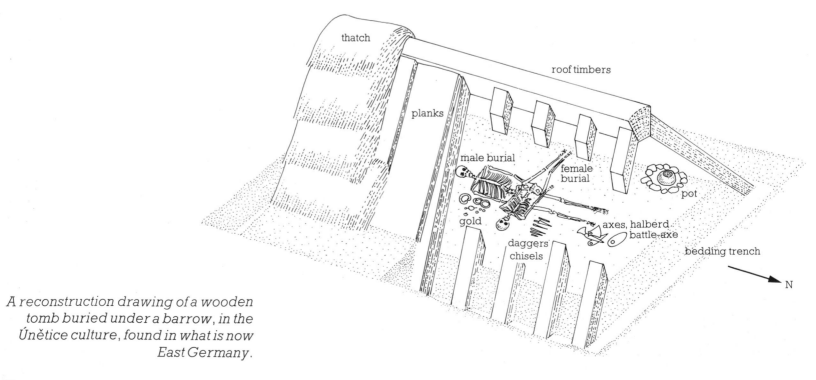

A reconstruction drawing of a wooden tomb buried under a barrow, in the Únětice culture, found in what is now East Germany.

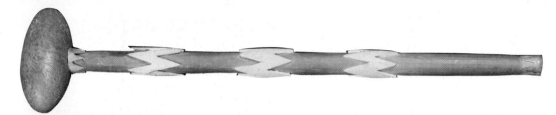

Sceptre from the Bush Barrow, Wessex Culture, Wiltshire.

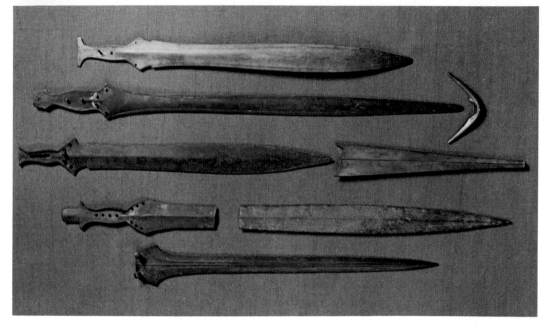

Swords and rapiers from the Bronze Age. Rivets and rivet holes show where wooden hilts were fixed to the blades.

powerful and wealthy. Most of the archaeological information about the Bronze Age comes from the burials of such aristocrats and from the bronze objects themselves.

In central Europe, for example, rich burials of the Únětice culture of 2000 to 1600 BC have been excavated, to show how the dead chieftain was buried lying down with a woman, perhaps a sacrificed wife, stretched across his lap. Surrounding him were golden necklets, pins and precious jewellery. He was also supplied with bronze daggers, chisels, axes and halberds (long-handled battle-axes). The grave was covered by a massive timber mortuary-house, which was then thatched. That in turn was covered by large stones and earth to make a high tumulus or mound. Centred in Czechoslovakia, the people of the Únětice culture mined the rich copper veins in Transylvania and are famous for their beautifully made bronze daggers and metal-shafted halberds. These have been found in places as far away as Denmark and Britain. Links with the distant Mediterranean are shown by colourful faience beads, made of a blue-green glass-like substance. They were produced and traded from Egypt and the Aegean and yet are found in Únětice graves.

At the same time, the Bronze Age civilizations described by the poet Homer were flourishing in the Aegean. The people of Troy, Mycenae and Crete lived in stone-walled towns, used chariots in warfare and produced great works of art. They represent the beginnings of the great classical civilizations of ancient Greece and Rome, yet still shared many of the traits of their barbarian neighbours in central and northern Europe. They had close ties with uncivilized peoples who they contacted in the course of trade. The close contact between the Mycenaean and the rich and powerful Wessex people in Britain is shown by the find of nearly identical bone-inlaid sceptres in the Bush Barrow burial of a Wessex chieftain in Wiltshire and in one of the royal graves at Mycenae itself.

New lands were opened up, for bronze axes were suitable for clearing woodland. Bronze weapons helped in the conquest of less developed peoples. Rapiers, developed as thrusting weapons, were a great improvement on the Wessex and Únětice daggers. Slashing swords with cutting edges on each side of the blade were invented. The Bronze Age was a period of great change and activity throughout Europe.

The Iron Age

Reconstruction of a circular Iron Age hut, Avoncroft, England.

The great Hittite civilization of central Anatolia kept secret its skills of iron ore smelting and iron-working for a long time. From about 1500 to 1200 BC the Hittites had exclusive control over iron tools and weapons. Then their empire collapsed under attack in about 1200 BC and their secret knowledge spread. Iron was a great improvement on bronze, especially for weapons. In the stories of Homer about Bronze Age Greece, we hear how famous warriors had to stop fighting to straighten out their bent bronze swords. Iron did not behave like that. By about 1000 BC iron was commonly used for tools in Greece and Italy. By the seventh and sixth centuries BC the knowledge of iron-working had spread throughout Europe. It was put to practical use while decorative work, including metal vessels and personal ornaments, were still made in bronze. This could be cast, hammered and inlaid easily. Iron working technology was confined to the hammering and wrought-iron techniques of the blacksmith.

Widespread demand for iron spearheads, swords, axes and hoes led to the development of the resources of iron and copper ore deposits in Austria, south Germany and Iberia. The warrior chiefs of these areas traded these raw materials to the Mediterranean city states. In return, they received luxury goods, such as classical bronze wine-mixing vessels, Greek painted pottery, bronze cauldrons on tripods and jars full of wine. Trading centres developed in northern and central Europe. Towns, such as the Heuneberg and Manching, both in Germany, were surrounded by rings of defensive banks, ditches and walls. On the shores of the Mediterranean, the Phoenicians set up colonies at Carthage (in Tunisia) and Tartessos (in Spain). The Greeks founded Marseilles and built ports in Sicily.

Iron Age Europe is famous for its superb artistic achievement in casting bronze and gold. Classical designs were adapted and changed into flowing abstract and zoomorphic (animal) designs. The two main periods of the Iron Age are known as the Hallstatt (700–450 BC) and the La Tène (450–1 BC), both based on changes in artistic style in metal working. In Britain, which was not occupied by the Romans until AD 43, development in style continued longer than in other parts of Europe. In Ireland, the Iron Age lasted until about AD 1000, where deeds of warrior chiefs were being written down by Celtic Christian monks.

It was not until much later that European blacksmiths developed the means to cast iron. This involves melting the metal completely and pouring it into a mould. In China, however, cast ironwork came before the discovery of hammering methods or wrought ironwork. In the seventh century BC farming implements and tools were skilfully cast, entailing the use of temperatures of at least 1835°C in the process. The high temperatures were probably possible because of the early development of very efficient

Huge Greek bronze vessel used for mixing wine, found in the grave of an Iron Age princess at Vix, France.

Bronze bucket, made in about 600 BC, from Hallstatt, Austria.

The walls of Great Zimbabwe, built AD 800 to 1500.

pottery kilns, constructed to fire porcelain. Wrought iron-work was only developed centuries later in China under the Han dynasty of 206 BC to AD 220.

Africa passed directly from the Stone Age to the Iron Age. The Kingdom of Meroë in the Sudan, which flourished from 395 BC to AD 350, was the centre of early iron-smelting in the Sahara. It probably derived its technology from Egypt which is revealed by evidence of Egyptian influences in its art.

Iron-working techniques probably reached West Africa from trading contacts with the North African coast. The people of the Nok culture in Nigeria were smelting and working iron by the third century BC. In East Africa, two streams of people who used iron gradually migrated south, east and west from the earliest Iron Age settlements of 300 BC around Lake Victoria. During the eleventh century AD, there was a rapid spread of peoples who worked and used iron, in Africa south of the Equator. At this time, several stone-walled trading centres with impressive architecture were built, such as Great Zimbabwe in Zimbabwe. Its labyrinthine walls surrounded a commercial and religious centre with far reaching connections.

Transport by Land and Sea

Rock engraving of prehistoric skiers, found in Sweden.

In the past three million years human beings have reached and populated most corners of the Earth. They have developed ways of life which allow them to live in the snow and ice of Arctic winters and in the hot, sandy deserts of the Kalahari. Most travelling has been done on foot. Sometimes it was over dry land that was only revealed during the Ice Ages when the level of the sea fell. It was in this way, perhaps as long ago as 40 000 BC, that the first inhabitants of the Americas arrived in Alaska. They travelled from northern Asia across the land bridge which spanned the Bering Straits.

The use of vehicles or pack animals seems necessary for transporting goods in bulk. But in some parts of the world, particularly in America before European colonization, most loads were carried by men and women. They used tumplines, or straps which run across the forehead or upper chest, attached to bundles or baskets which they carried on their backs. The use of wheels and pack animals was unknown to them. In Mesopotamia, domesticated oxen drew two- and four-wheeled carts and wagons in 3500 BC. Chariots with spoked wheels were drawn by horses in Anatolia two thousand years later. In the far North, in 2000 BC, Arctic hunters were following their prey on skis, transporting tents and domestic equipment on large sledges pulled by dogs.

There are parts of the world, such as the islands of the

Gold model of a Persian war-chariot, made in about 500 BC.

Silver model of a boat found at Ur, and made in about 2500 BC.

Pacific Ocean, which could not have been reached without the use of sea-going craft. We do not know when people first took to the water. But those living near rivers and lakes may have known how to swim and used logs or inflated animal skins to float on. Only a very few early boats have been found and excavated. A dug-out boat, dated by the carbon 14 method to 6400 BC, was found at Pesse in northern Holland. It had been made by hollowing out a tree trunk.

Paintings and engravings sometimes show boats, but they are often too simplified to tell the archaeologist much about their construction. Some pictures, however, such as wall-paintings in Egyptian tombs, give much detailed information. At about 3000 BC Egyptian boats were made of bundles of papyrus reeds tied together and paddled along. By 2500 BC the Egyptians were building sea-worthy wooden ships with single, square sails. Rafts were used to ferry large, heavy loads such as huge stone blocks used in building temples and pyramids. In Scandinavia, rock engravings show small kayaks, rather like canoes, and oval corracles made from animal skins stretched over wooden frames. Large boats, powered by as many as thirty oars, were sailing on the Mediterranean by 2500 BC and similar vessels are shown on Danish carvings a thousand years later.

In order to discover how early craft were navigated, exciting experiments have been carried out. Thor Heyerdahl led an expedition to sail the famous balsa log raft, *Kon Tiki*, from the mainland of South America to Polynesia in the South Pacific. This was to prove such a voyage was possible. Similar pottery styles and the presence of similar words in the languages of the two areas hinted at long-distance sea contact at an early date. In 1978 a leather boat was made according to descriptions in medieval documents. It was sailed across the Atlantic from Ireland to North America in order to show that there might be some truth in the legend that St Brendan had discovered America!

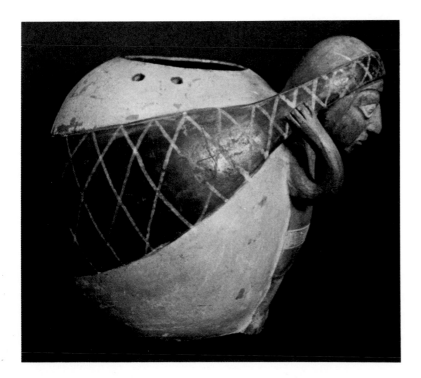

Moche pot of a Peruvian Indian using a tumpline to carry a load, made between AD 200 and 700.

Evidence from Coins

Coins were first invented about 630 BC in Lydia in Turkey. Ever since then, people have been losing them and coins turn up in archaeological excavations. Sometimes they were lost accidentally. They fell from purses or pockets while people were in markets, walking down streets, or fording streams. At other times hoards of coins were hidden to keep them safe in times of trouble and the owners never returned to find them. Occasionally, however, they were buried for a different reason. The great Anglo-Saxon ship burial at Sutton Hoo contained a purse holding thirty-seven small gold coins, three circular blanks and two small bars of gold. Perhaps these were placed there to pay each member of the ghostly crew of the ship!

Coins are struck or cast from metal, often gold or silver. This has helped to preserve them if they are buried in the earth, because these metals do not corrode easily. In the earliest days of coinage, each Greek city issued its own coins, usually marked on one side with an emblem symbolizing the gods who protected the city, such as the owl for Athena and Athens. At a later period, rulers began to

Silver tetradrachm (four-drachma piece) from Athens, minted in 440–430 BC.

place their portrait, the date of minting and claims to power on coins, a practice continued to the present day.

Finds of coins are valuable to the archaeologist in several ways. They can reveal links between the site where they

Copper ingot probably used as currency in Zambia in the fourteenth century AD.

In the third century BC, the Celtic tribes of northwestern Europe began to copy the gold coinage of Macedonia, shown at the top. Gradually, the classical design of a portrait head and horse-drawn chariot became stylized beyond recognition, as these Celtic coins, middle and bottom, show.

Coins which have been made from a mixture of gold or silver with less precious metals show a weak economy and possibly civil unrest. On the other hand, the fact that coinage of pure quality was being minted frequently tells us that the economy was stable and the rulers powerful.

It is difficult to say if the coins found in a hoard are a typical sample of those which were in circulation at the time the hoard was collected. Sometimes this may be so, and the coins will be found to match the pattern of coins built up from isolated finds. At other times, the hoard may contain mainly old or high value coins. This would suggest that it may have been one person's or a family's savings, built up over a number of years.

Coins make the exchange of goods and services easier. They help us to place a common set of values on a wide range of different things. They obviously aid the growth of urban and trading societies. But people have managed without them in many parts of the world. Coins were unknown in the Aztec and Inca Empires before the Spaniards arrived. In many parts of New Guinea they are still not used. This does not mean that these areas lacked 'currency', or special items which could be exchanged for a set number of articles. It is probable that in the European Stone Age, stone axe heads were used in this way. In Africa, copper ingots from the Congo area were widely traded in the period before European contact. In many areas useful items, such as axe or knife blades and fish hooks, became elaborated so that they were no longer of practical use. They served as tokens used only for the exchange of certain sorts of goods.

were found and other places. The Sutton Hoo coins can all be shown to come from areas ruled by the Merovingian Franks (the earliest French kings) in the seventh century AD. Also coins can usually be dated and so indicate the earliest time at which they could have been deposited. Of course, you have to be careful with isolated finds. A Roman coin dug up in Ecuador does not prove the Romans reached South America! Coins can demonstrate long distance contacts as well. For example, many coins are copies of others. The gold *staters* of Phillip II (who reigned from 359 to 336 BC) and Alexander III (who reigned from 336 to 323 BC) of Macedon, rulers of a country of the ancient world, north of Greece, were widely imitated by the Celts in northern Europe. The Celts gradually broke down the original designs and remade them into abstract patterns.

Analysis of the metal in coins can also indicate something of the political conditions under which they were made.

Weapons and War

People have always shown an unparalleled willingness to destroy each other. There are countless remains of weapons and victims to prove it. Weapons may first have originated as hunting tools. Perhaps they were turned against other human beings over claims to property, food or land. By looking at the shape of weapons we can trace how they developed. Many different kinds of weapons grew from the simple chopper tools and handaxes of the Old Stone Age. By 10 000 BC there were numerous specialized weapons, such as flaked stone arrow heads, spears with stone or hardened wood points and bone harpoons.

Weapons turn up in many sites, although usually only the inorganic parts are well preserved. Thus metal sword blades and stone projectile heads from spears and arrows are recovered, sling or catapult shot, or iron bolts fired from Roman or medieval siege engines. The wooden sword grips, arrow shafts and catapult machinery have long since rotted in the soil. In later sites guns may be found, especially bronze, brass and iron cannon and the shot they fired. Iron cannon balls are sometimes still embedded in the masonry against which they were used. The spread of firearms into new areas may be traced by other remains.

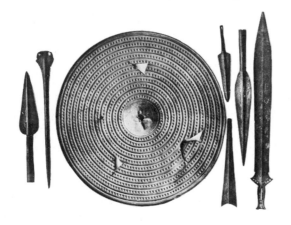

Circular bronze parade shield, sword, dagger, rapier and spear heads, found in the River Thames and dated 1000–5000 BC.

Greek bronze statuette of a helmeted warrior on horseback, made about 550 BC.

The impressive hillfort of Maiden Castle was defended by British warriors against the invading Romans. Some of the slain were found buried near the intricate eastern gateway.

Rectangular Norfolk flints, used in the locks of guns imported during the past few hundred years, are found all over West Africa, long after the guns themselves have disappeared. Some archaeologists have tried to test the efficiency of ancient weapons. For example, a model of a Roman ballista, a military engine for hurling metal bolts, was made to test its range and speed of working. It proved extremely efficient!

It is impossible to say what proportion of the human race has been destroyed by warfare. But a few of the victims of war are sometimes discovered by archaeologists. The Iron Age fort of Maiden Castle in Dorset was stormed by the Roman army in about AD 43. Excavations inside the huge earthwork defences revealed the skeletons of thirty-eight Britons buried hastily during the assault. They still wore bronze anklets and toe rings which showed that they were humble warriors and not great lords. The slashing cuts of swords, stabs from legionaries' short swords, and small, square holes in skulls made by throwing spears revealed the devastating effect of Roman weapons. One man was found with the remains of an iron ballista bolt still embedded in his spine. Nearby 20 000 sling shots were found, stacked ready for use against the invading forces.

The effects of weapons and warfare are reflected in a variety of ways. New weapons led to new systems of defence and may have caused men to abandon the territory they already held. Groups of people found it necessary to build elaborate defences, such as the massive stone walls encircling many medieval towns. They had to modify their style of building; castle architecture changed when cannon began to be used. Round towers replaced square ones, which could easily be demolished by firing at their corners. Sometimes the relation between weapons, warfare and changes in architecture is more indirect. It was the absence of war, partly due to the increase in royal power, which led to the disappearance of the English fortified manor house in the sixteenth and seventeenth centuries.

The introduction of the stirrup into Europe led to the development of cavalry who could fight against each other on horseback. This helped to alter the whole pattern of European military tactics and led to pitched battles on level ground.

Magic and Religion

Reconstruction of a ceremony at Çatal Hüyük, about 6150 BC. Priestesses are dressed as vultures, and make offerings to a large bull's head.

We do not know when religious beliefs and activities first began. Neanderthalers, 50 000 years ago, buried their dead in graves with flowers. This suggests some sort of belief that physical death was not a complete end. *Homo erectus* at Chou K'ou Tien, China, may have eaten human flesh, as the evidence from bones suggests. It may have been part of a ceremony to appease the spirits of the dead, to gain the power of the dead person, or simply out of affection.

By the time that the first cities began to develop, evidence for religious beliefs becomes clearer. A shrine dating from about 6000 BC was found at Çatal Hüyük, Turkey, in which human skulls were placed near to large modelled bulls' heads. In Jericho, human skulls with features modelled in plaster and shell-inlaid eyes, made about 7000 BC, may show that the townspeople revered their ancestors.

Nearly all archaeological evidence about religion and ritual is difficult to interpret. We cannot easily or safely reconstruct what human beings believed in from material remains alone. When we excavate a ninth century Anglo-Saxon church or a Hindu temple, we can form some idea of the ceremonies performed in it and the beliefs behind

them. But this is because these are temples of religions and traditions which still exist. When we excavate great Maya ceremonial centres in Central America, however, we can do little more than guess at the details of the rituals once held there. But from the pictures of the gods carved on temple walls, we can tell that our ancestors worshipped forces that were vital to their lives, such as the Sun, Moon, rain, and the fertility of the land.

Many female figurines made of clay or stone are found in archaeological sites. Some archaeologists have taken these as evidence of a widespread cult of a 'mother goddess', possibly associated with ideas of fertility. Others have suggested these may have had a variety of uses, perhaps as dolls or memorials to dead women. Maybe they were simply intended to show ideal feminine beauty. We will never know for certain what the owner believed about them.

Where written evidence exists the matter is far easier. As writing developed, professional priests emerged in many towns and cities. Their inscriptions in temples or on tablets may throw light on beliefs and practices. Therefore, we can learn a great deal from writings about the

Asshur, chief of all the Assyrian gods.

Ganesha, worshipped in Hinduism.

The Willendorf Venus, 40 000 BC.

religion of Mesopotamia and ancient Egypt, the names of their gods and their special powers. Occasionally, archaeology may also show how writings of the time have not revealed all the actual religious beliefs. At Ur, in Mesopotamia, graves were discovered dating from about 2500 BC. Queen Shub-ad lay in one of these, elaborately ornamented. With her were her priests, soldiers and a wagon pulled by asses, its drivers and all her ladies in waiting who had accompanied her into death. No one had suspected such burials from religious texts written at the time.

We can also gain an idea of beliefs from the objects left at shrines as offerings. Sometimes they indicate that some particular kind of help was wanted. At the Roman temple at the source of the River Seine in France, models of parts of the human body were found. Worshippers left hands and feet made of clay showing rheumatism and little busts of people with goitre, eye infections and symptoms of mental illness. They hoped the god of healing would cure them of these illnesses. Objects from the Roman temple at Lydney Park, Gloucester, have also been interpreted as showing the god's concern with healing and hunting.

A decorated human skull from Jericho.

Graves and Tombs

Death has always been regarded as more than just the end of life. Many peoples believe that after death the spirit lives on, even if only for a short time. When death occurs it is usually dealt with by a religious or magical ceremony. Part of this will be concerned with disposing of the body of the deceased. How the dead person is treated depends very much on his or her position while alive. The poor, the young and the unimportant usually receive far less attention than the rich and powerful.

The human practice of disposing of the dead in a ceremonial way is of great use to archaeologists. Burials or cremations not only provide them with skeletal remains, but often include grave goods which relate in some way to the life of the individuals.

It is natural that the spectacular burials of the aristocracy should have attracted most popular attention. Probably the most famous of these is the tomb of Tutankhamun, a young Egyptian king of the fourteenth century BC, excavated in the 1920s. The tomb, which contained the mummified body of Tutankhamun himself, had largely escaped the attention of ancient tomb robbers. It revealed the incredible wealth with which the Egyptians surrounded their pharaohs. There were chariots covered with gold and bronze, alabaster vases and even containers filled with food, such as roast duck, for his afterlife. Almost as impressive are the tombs of the Bronze Age Zhou (Chou) dynasty in China, dating from 1027 to 475 BC, in which, at the bottom of a pit, men were buried near chariots and the horses used to pull them.

In many cultures, important burials are covered with large mounds or barrows. This indicates the amount of labour which could be organized and channelled into commemorating the society's leaders. One of the most puzzling of such burials is the extremely rich ship burial at Sutton Hoo in England. It does not seem to contain any human remains, although they may have disintegrated in the acid soil. Perhaps it was a pagan commemoration of a king whose body had not been rescued. The grave goods reveal a mixture of pagan and Christian beliefs. Perhaps

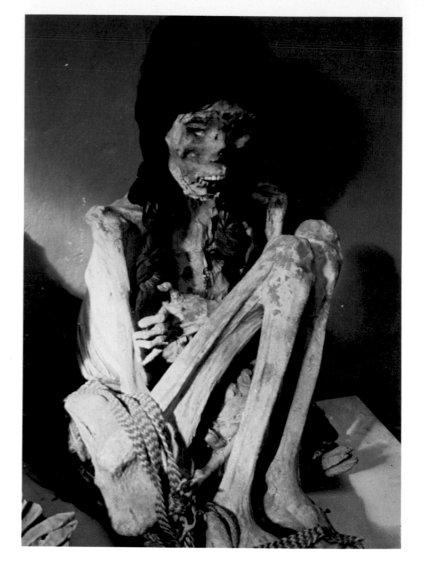

The dry sand of the Atacama desert, Chile, has preserved the hair and skin of this body for hundreds of years.

the king had been converted to Christianity, lapsed back into paganism, and been given a mixed pagan and Christian burial.

Humbler burials can also provide a great deal of information. Cemetery sites need careful excavation, for burials may have intruded into earlier layers. Cremations are also informative. The remains are usually placed in special containers which often indicate the dead person's homeland. Scientific examination of the skeletons can indicate the ages at which people died or were killed, how

Tattoo of a deer with an eagle's beak and long antlers, found on the right arm of the chief buried in a barrow, at Pazyryk, USSR.

many men and women in a group, and the diseases from which they suffered. Grave goods can indicate their trading links and the kind of jewellery and clothes they would have owned when they were alive.

In some parts of the world, the weather conditions under which corpses are disposed of helps preserve the flesh of the bodies. The dry, desert climate of parts of coastal Peru leads to a natural mummification of bodies, leaving flesh and hair almost intact. The burials at Pazyryk in the Altai Mountains, Siberia, were preserved by intense cold which helped seal them completely. Many leather, cloth and wooden items were found in a remarkable state of preservation after 2500 years. Large pieces of human skin, some of it elaborately tattooed, were also recovered.

A single group of people may dispose of its dead in several different ways. In West Africa today, for example, priests may be interred under the floors of their homes. The bones of kings are kept in special mausolea. Ordinary people are buried in coffins in areas of a village cemetery reserved for their clan or family. In the past slaves were buried without coffins away from the main cemetery, and young children and convicted criminals tumbled into very shallow graves in the village rubbish dump!

Part of the funeral treasure of Tutankhamun.

Home Life

Did Stone Age mothers sing lullabies to their children? We shall never know. But we may get a good idea of where they sat while they nursed them, by examining in detail the things they dropped on the floor of their living areas. A pattern can be worked out from finds, such as spindle whorls and needles, or broken tools and weapons, which shows what went on in different parts of the home. This often indicates if areas were usually occupied by women or men. Excavations of a hunter's camp in northern France showed how, at about 10 000 BC, flint knapping (chipping) was done near to the fireplace. From the way the waste flakes of stone lay in the archaeological layers, it was possible to tell that the flint worker always sat with his or her back or side to the fire. Other excavations have shown definite areas for sleeping and preparing food.

At Skara Brae in the Orkney Isles, a complete Neolithic village was discovered after a violent storm had blown away the sand dune which covered it for 4000 years. Wood was very scarce, so the villagers used stone to build and furnish their houses. Their small rectangular rooms were linked by covered, stone passageways which protected the people from the harsh weather. Cupboards, shelves and box beds were built of stone slabs set into the drystone walls. Their bedding was probably dried grass or heather. Stone water tanks in the floor may have contained live fish kept for food when the sea was too rough to venture out.

Human beings have lived in a vast variety of houses and

The site at Skara Brae, Orkney, where stone built and furnished Neolithic houses look out across the North Atlantic.

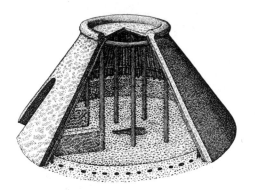

Archaeologists have been able to reconstruct many types of ancient dwellings. The hut shown far left was made from mammoth bones, poles and hide in the Ukraine, 70 000 to 30 000 years ago. The houses shown centre and right are from Pan P'o, a Neolithic village dated 4000 BC, in Shensi Province, China.

shelters. These range from the small domed mud-brick houses of the early Neolithic people of Cyprus, to the well-known wooden long-houses of the Vikings. All buildings, where enough evidence survives, show a deliberate arrangement of rooms or living areas. This suggests that the people who lived there felt that particular places were right for particular tasks. Groups of simple Maya one-roomed houses have been excavated. They were built on raised mounds around the edge of a plaza. They show that some were used only for cooking, some for sleeping, and others, usually the grandest or biggest, were small shrines with decorated walls, where the gods of rain or the Moon may have been worshipped.

In many dwellings the fire, the centre of domestic life and food preparation, seems to have been the most important area of the home and the point from which everything else radiated. Even where there are no walls, for example in a hunter's camp, fires mark out divisions within a large group. Among modern Bushmen of the Kalahari Desert, even the most temporary camp is given a basic division by erecting simple marker posts. Each fire forms the centre of separate families or kin groups, and a person may not walk casually from one fire to another. This kind of regulation may well have applied to Stone Age hunters and gatherers.

In early societies, most things needed by the family were made at home, rather than bartered or bought from specialist craftsmen. Clothes, cooking utensils and tools were among the most important things produced. Usually men were the tool-makers, but men or women may have made pottery, prepared skins or woven cloth. Archaeologists can usually only guess at what kind of clothes prehistoric people wore. The cloth and skin have usually rotted away, leaving only the fastenings. Most clothes were simple wrap-around garments held in place by ties or thongs, belts, brooches or pins. Remains of spindle whorls, loom weights and bone weaving combs and needles give clues to weaving techniques. Special stone tools, such as scrapers, and bone needles are evidence that skin and fur were prepared and used for clothing and bedding.

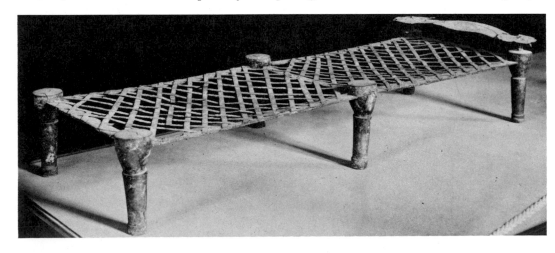

A bronze bed made by the Etruscans, about 350 BC.

Toys and Games

Many doll-like figurines and models of animals, houses, furniture and vehicles have been found in archaeological excavations. To us they look like toys, but to the people who made them, they had a very different meaning. Most of these finds come from the graves of adults, not children, and there is the major clue. These miniature objects were put into the grave or tomb as grave goods, which the dead person would be able to use in the afterlife.

Some wealthy people, such as Tutankhamun, Queen Shub-ad of Sumeria, and Chinese princes and princesses, were buried with all their priceless jewels, household goods and sometimes even their servants. Less important people had to make do with models of these things, which were considered to be just as good as the real thing. At about 3000 BC pottery models of log-built houses were made in central Europe. Many clay models of four-wheeled carts have been found in graves in Transylvania. In China, long processions of figurines, some mounted on horseback, wound around tombs.

Some real toys, however, have survived to the present day. The dry sands of Egypt have preserved roughly made rag dolls, painted wooden animals on wheels, and stone mice with moveable jaws and tails. One of the oldest and most complicated toys, made in Egypt at about 1900 BC, is a set of small ivory dwarfs fitted on to a box. The dwarfs are set dancing by pulling strings. The ancient Greeks and Romans also made toys for their children. At about 400 BC they played with jointed wooden and clay dolls. A very cleverly designed clay doll was made, which mimicked the actions of a woman rolling out pastry with a rolling pin. Roman children played with armies of lead soldiers just as modern children do. Paintings on vases show Greek children playing with balls, and tops and whips, over 2000 years ago.

Games were played by both children and adults. One of the most popular games of the classical world was called Knucklebones. It was similar to modern Five Stones. The pieces were originally small bones from the ankle joints of cloven-footed animals, such as sheep and goats. But

Girl on a swing: an ingenious toy made about 1500 BC on the island of Crete.

many copies were made in ivory, wood or stone. The game was to throw the knucklebones up into the air and try to catch them on the back of the hand. Knucklebones were also used as dice, though the modern kind of six-sided die was also known to the Greeks and Romans. Each knucklebone had four differently moulded sides, each of which had a different value. Four knucklebones were thrown at a time and the scores were added up. Many combinations of values had nicknames such as 'Old Woman' and 'Aphrodite'. Counters were used with knucklebones to play a kind of backgammon. Some counters had inscriptions on them saying MALE(E)ST (bad luck) or VICTOR (winner).

Several gaming boards have survived for 5000 years. Unfortunately, the rules have not. Five gaming boards of about 3000 BC were found in the royal graves at Ur. The most beautiful of these is completely covered with shell plaques inlaid with brilliant blue lapis lazuli and red lime-

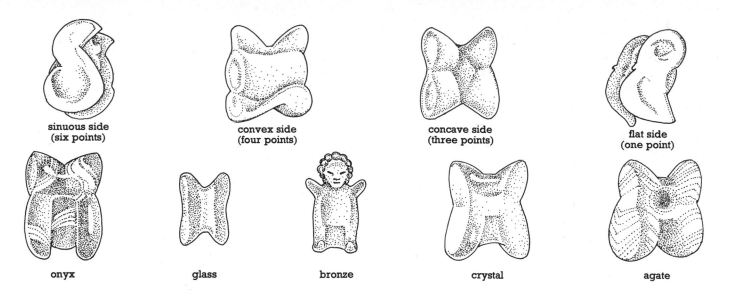

**sinuous side
(six points)**

**convex side
(four points)**

**concave side
(three points)**

**flat side
(one point)**

onyx

glass

bronze

crystal

agate

stone. The board is hollow and contained the counters and dice. There are seven white and seven black counters and three white and three blue pyramid-shaped dice. The ancient Egyptians played a game called Senet on a very similar board. This game is shown on a wall-painting dated 2600 BC, and a complete gaming set from about 1500 BC has been found. Like the Sumerian game, the board is hollow and contained the pieces, but it also has another game marked out on the reverse side. For the second game, the board was marked with three columns of ten

Knucklebones were sometimes used as dice. Four were thrown at once and the score added up. Each bone has four sides which score different numbers of points. Special knucklebones were made from semi-precious stones, bronze or glass.

squares. Two sets of ten men were used; one set was spool-shaped, the other conical. Both Senet and the Game of Thirty Squares were very important to the ancient Egyptians, who believed that the spirits of the dead played these games in the afterlife.

One of the gaming boards found at Ur, with round counters and dice.

Recreating the Past

All archaeology is an attempt to reconstruct part of the past. The archaeologist takes the information and objects he recovers from the earth, and uses his skills and imagination to bring them to life. Making models or drawing pictures can show us vanished worlds. They can also suggest new lines of enquiry to the archaeologist, who may not have considered certain points of construction or detail.

The best archaeological artists are those who have a firm understanding of the sites they illustrate. They show how ruined houses, castles and temples might have looked where people once lived, worked, fought and worshipped. People are always included in reconstruction drawings to give us an idea of the scale of the buildings. The scene is drawn from a bird's eye view to create an impression of the whole site.

Carefully built scale-models help to change a complicated archaeological site into a three-dimensional form which can be easily understood. But sometimes full-scale, real life reconstructions are made. On Easter Island, isolated in the South Pacific Ocean, the famous voyager Thor Heyerdahl led an investigation into how the island's huge stone figures were quarried, moved several kilometres to their final site, and then erected on stone platforms. Using the advice and labour of native Easter Islanders and having studied unfinished statues in the quarries, he completed one figure by using old stone picks to chip away the rock.

One hundred and eighty Easter Islanders dragged the statue to its site. It did not take as many people to actually raise it. Twelve men with poles levered the statue, while

Preparing a meal under Iron Age conditions.

View of the Iron Age settlement built on the Dorset–Wiltshire border for the 'Living in the Past' experiment.

Two crushed harps dating from 2750 BC, revealed during the excavation of the Death Pit at Ur.

The completed reconstruction of the smaller instrument

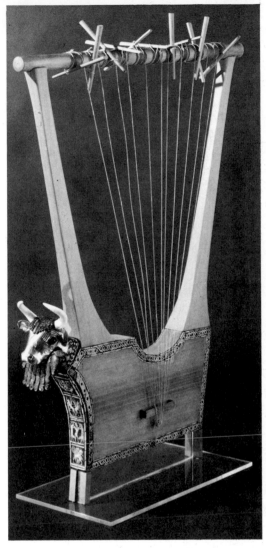

another man slipped pebbles and larger stones underneath to build up a wedge-shaped ramp. After eighteen days of painstaking work the statue fell into its prepared base. From this reconstruction exercise, Heyerdahl was able to calculate the labour and time involved in such a project. He drew conclusions about the original inhabitants and their society between AD 1000 and 1700 when the other statues were put in place. There must have been very powerful chiefs to organize the hundreds of stone-carvers and labourers involved in producing and erecting all these great stone giants.

Perhaps the most moving reconstructions are those of musical instruments. After hundreds or even thousands of years, we can hear once again the sounds which delighted long-dead priests and kings. The completely squashed remains of a shell inlaid harp, with a wonderful bull's head in gold, its eyes, beard and horn-tips of lapis lazuli, were found in the Sumerian royal graves at Ur. It has been put back together again with painstaking detective work. A stringed instrument from the Sutton Hoo ship burial has been remade in two different ways, as a harp and as a lyre. It has been played in public to accompany recitations of the great Anglo-Saxon poem, *Beowulf*.

Sometimes reconstructions are on a grand scale. Ruined buildings and whole sites are cleared and rebuilt to show them at their finest time. The great Maya city of Tikal in Guatemala was carefully cleared of jungle which had invaded it and caused stelae (upright slabs) and masonry to fall. Many years of excavation work followed. An equally long time was spent on replacing stone blocks, reinforcing dangerous walls and recreating the architecture of the enormous pyramid temples.

The most elaborate reconstructions are those which depend upon repopulating the reconstructed sites with living people and animals. In 1977 a group of English people volunteered to live in Iron Age conditions, with virtually no contact with the modern world, for a whole year. They survived, with only a few drop-outs, but none would care to repeat the experiment!

The Story in Pictures

We must use our imagination to interpret the remains of the past. Here and there in our finds we discover pictures and images – paintings, engravings, carvings and castings – which show something of life in the societies in which they were made. Sometimes we can learn a lot from these. More often they raise more questions than they answer.

In the nineteenth century, the great cave paintings of the Old Stone Age were rediscovered. They had been preserved almost perfectly underground for 20 000 years or more. The public was startled and puzzled, for here was a sophisticated art which seemed to date back to Mankind's earliest days. We still do not know how art began. Nor are we very sure what we can learn from the cave paintings. There are many theories about them and especially about the animals many of them depict, the bison, horses, mammoths and reindeer. Perhaps they were painted for the joy of self-expression and no more. Were they magical to ensure success in hunting? Some pictures show wounded animals and what seem to be spear or arrow marks. Or perhaps the paintings were intended to encourage animals to breed and multiply. Maybe their makers, like the Australian Aborigines, revered them as totems, or symbols, of their tribe. No one is sure of the truth, for we cannot test these theories.

Recently, archaeologists have examined how frequently certain types of painting, such as horses, bison, and of various abstract signs, like wavy lines and geometric shapes, occur in caves. They have pointed out how certain animals and abstract signs are grouped together in various wall-paintings.

The fact that artists create images does not mean that those images can automatically be understood by people from other ages. To interpret pictures or sculptures, the archaeologist must try to judge what the image meant to its makers, its relationship to other works of art and its age. By studying where an image was used it is possible to get some broad idea of its purpose. Pictures on funerary pots or in tombs may have a special meaning. They may seem to show scenes of everyday life, but really depict

The Mimbres potters of New Mexico, AD 1000–1200, made pots such as this for use as grave goods.

stories of the gods. But what is the meaning of the Folkton Drums? These are three chalk cylinders found in a child's grave in north Yorkshire and carved with highly stylized faces. Who are the curious creatures painted inside the beautiful Mimbres pots of New Mexico? There are many mysteries we shall probably never understand.

Some pictures, fortunately, tell us a little more. The great carved stone friezes from Assyria show scenes of lion-hunting, battles and ceremonial processions. They illuminate that society's life even though they show only the nobility and not the ordinary people. The pictures on

Two of the Folkton Drums.

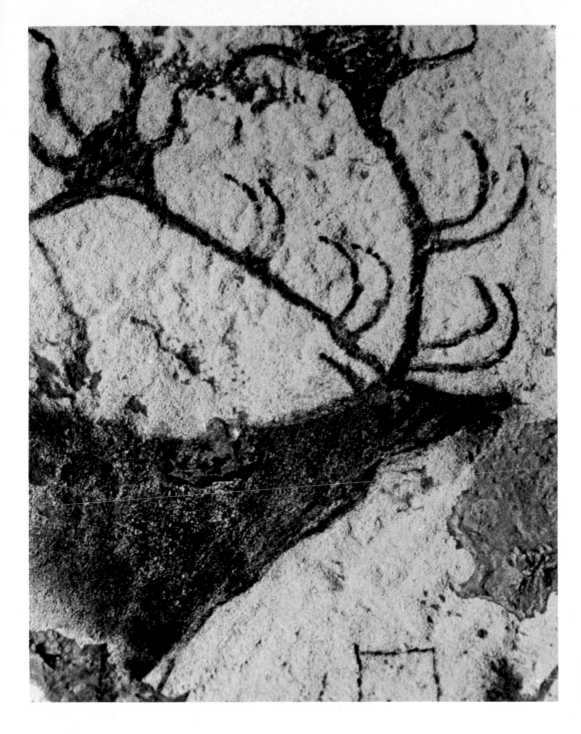

Old Stone Age cave painting of a stag and a rectangular shape, discovered at Lascaux, France.

Maya temples, painted pots and stelae can also be interpreted. They portray grand processions and sacrifices. The paintings on the pots of the Moche people of Peru show many everyday scenes such as fishing or hunting. Perhaps they are really about mythical gods and heroes.

In dealing with pictures archaeologists have to be cautious. They must consider the circumstances in which they were found and compare them with others from similar sites. Above all they must never try to force a meaning on them. Archaeologists, unlike anthropologists, cannot talk to the people they study. Their information always comes from the past to the present. Archaeologists must accept that they may never be able to understand with certainty some of the messages.

Treasure Hunters

Throughout the ages people have dreamt of finding buried treasure. The knowledge that previous generations buried their dead with rich grave goods, or that once famous cities are now lost, drives people to search and, occasionally, to find. Sometimes this has led to spectacular archaeological discoveries. More often than not it has ruined important sites and led to the destruction of valuable evidence. Today treasure hunting, grave robbing and illegal excavation are flourishing as never before in many parts of the world.

Many of the first antiquarians were spurred on by the desire to make spectacular discoveries and to keep what they found for themselves. In the eighteenth and early nineteenth centuries, it was a favourite pastime to dig into ancient burial mounds to see what could be found. Several might be dug in a single day. Those which contained nothing attractive or beautiful were considered worthless. Unwanted material was dumped. Little or no attempt was made to record the finds or digging operations. Objects recovered in this way are now to be found in many public collections. But they are almost useless because no proper notes were kept about their discovery.

Between 1815 and 1819 Belzoni, a giant ex-circus strongman, smashed his way into Egyptian tombs. He removed the more striking or saleable objects, including some remarkable mummies, and abandoned or destroyed the rest. Heinrich Schliemann, who rediscovered the ancient city of Troy, smuggled out some of his most precious finds under his wife's skirt!

Towards the end of the last century, archaeologists began to turn their attention away from hunting for treasures with which to astonish the world and ensure their fame. They started to concentrate on increasing their knowledge of the past. To do this they realized that they must methodically recover everything they could from the earth, and carefully record and publish their excavations. Then other scholars could study and, if necessary, correct their interpretations.

Unfortunately, as archaeology has developed and

Sophia Schliemann wearing the 'jewels of Helen' found at Troy in 1873.

become more widely publicized, many people wish to own archaeological pieces simply because they are rare or beautiful and their possession brings pleasure. Today this desire keeps treasure hunters, grave robbers and fakers in business in many parts of the world.

Customers will pay well for beautiful or rare treasures, however they have come on to the market. In many parts of Latin America professional looters, called *guaqueros*, are highly skilled at detecting ancient burial sites from which they remove goldwork, pottery and cloth. The sites are dug quickly and crudely and much valuable evidence is destroyed forever. Some looters are highly

Belzoni hauled away massive sculptures from ancient Egyptian sites, as well as taking many smaller treasures.

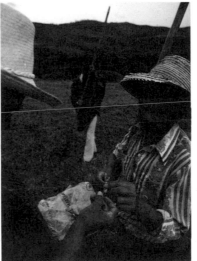

Crowds gathered to watch Heinrich Schliemann's excavation of the royal graves at Mycenae, Greece.

Colombian tomb-robbers inspect the gold objects they have looted.

organized and violent. Planes and helicopters have been used to fly out pieces of carved stone sliced off Maya stelae hidden in the jungle. Many crucial inscriptions have been defaced or destroyed. Some of those who have tried to prevent this have been murdered. The problem is almost world-wide. In Ghana, funerary sites rich in terracotta human heads representing ancestors, were secretly located and stripped. The figurines were sold to dealers. In Italy, Etruscan tombs have been robbed of their contents and their murals.

The archaeologist loathes treasure hunting. It destroys evidence and thrives on the greed some people have to possess things and make money out of antiquities. Many countries have passed laws to stop unofficial excavations. Steps have been taken to stop items illegally obtained from being taken from one country to another. However, the problem continues, and metal detectors have recently made the problem worse. Amateur treasure hunters, encouraged by well-publicized stories of finds of coins or precious metals, dig where they will and often keep or sell anything they find. It is, therefore, very important for us to realize how much harm is done by such illegal activity. We must treasure what should be everyone's to see and enjoy.

Gold and Goldsmiths

The gleam of gold has always fascinated Mankind. It is a noble metal that never tarnishes and glitters in river sands and in veined quartz. It was probably the first metal to be discovered and used. Nuggets the size of peas, or even bigger, could easily be collected from river gravels and treasured as they were or worked into ornamental shapes.

By about 4000 BC the people of Mesopotamia had discovered one of the curious properties of gold. Unlike other metals, it does not become brittle and crack when it is hammered, but can be beaten into thin sheets. In Peru, a goldsmith's grave dated to about 2000 BC shows us that, there too, gold nuggets were being hammered flat using smooth river pebbles. The earliest ornaments were made by cutting gold sheet to shape and by decorating it with shallow engravings. Sometimes designs were hammered out from the back of the sheet to make slightly raised, *repoussé* ornaments. Bowls, helmets and cups were made by beating gold sheet over shaped wooden, stone or resin moulds or templates.

In the ancient world gold was used mainly for making personal ornaments. It was also used for making special ceremonial objects, such as precious cups, sceptres and masks to be put over the faces of dead kings or chiefs. Only the ancient Colombian Indians used gold for making such everyday objects as fish-hooks, chisels and tweezers. From about 600 BC gold, silver and a naturally occurring alloy of the two, electrum, were used to make the world's first coins. These circulated in the Mediterranean area and were used in the wine and olive oil trade.

Gold is often found as a pure metal. Therefore, unlike copper and iron, there is no need for complicated smelting processes. The nuggets or grains simply have to be melted at a temperature of 1063°C. This kind of heat could be produced by using a hollow cane as a blow pipe and blowing air onto glowing charcoal, or later in furnaces with draughts provided by bellows. Not all the gold we see in museums is pure gold. It was soon discovered that a mixture of 80 per cent gold to 20 per cent copper produced an alloy with all the colour and quality of gold, but with a much lower melting point. This made the casting of gold ornaments much easier. Rounded, three-dimensional gold objects could be made using moulds, and then decorated using other goldworking techniques such as filigree and granulation. In filigree work, gold strips were made into gold wire by drawing them through different shaped perforations. It was then bent into shape on the back plate, formed into borders, spirals and curves, and soldered into place. For granulation, small spherical drops of gold, or granules, could be made by dropping molten gold into cold water, where it solidified. The tiny granules were also soldered into position. It is amazing how delicate the work is when you consider that ancient goldsmiths had no electricity or magnifying glasses to help them.

Many peoples in different parts of the world have used the lost-wax method, or *cire perdue*, for casting complicated gold ornaments. The Sumerians used this ingenious technique as early as 2800 BC. The ancient goldsmiths of Colombia and Ecuador were producing charm-like animal pendants in this way by about 500 BC.

Stages in making a hollow gold frog ornament using the lost-wax method, and the finished object.

clay core

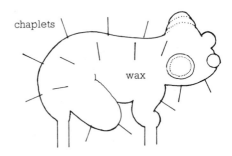

chaplets

wax

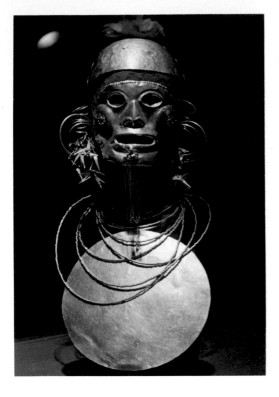

Gold torc, or neck-ring, from Snettisham, Norfolk, about 100 BC.

Gold and lapis lazuli jewellery from the Death Pit at Ur, about 2750 BC.

A helmet, face-mask and jewellery made of a gold and copper alloy, found in Colombia and dated about AD 1100.

The object desired in gold was first modelled in beeswax over a clay core. It was then decorated with coils of fine wax threads and details such as eyes and hair were added. The wax model was in turn covered with clay, which was allowed to harden. When hard, the whole thing was heated, the wax melted and poured out through specially made tubes, or chaplets, leaving a hole in the clay coating. Next, the molten gold was poured into the empty space and allowed to solidify and cool. Then the clay mould was broken to reveal the golden object inside. Finally, it would be cleaned and polished using fine sand, smooth pebbles and bone tools.

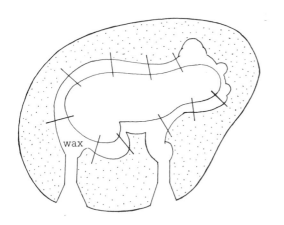

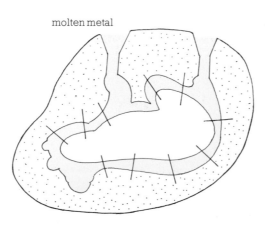

Myths, Legends and Reality

To help them understand the distant past many societies have developed myths and legends. Archaeologists continually strive to break through these myths and grasp the past as it really was. Occasionally, they find that a few of them contain cores of truth.

Perhaps the most appealing and widespread myths are those which recount the existence of a former golden age. One such myth is that of Atlantis. It was mentioned by the Greek philosopher Plato as a great civilization, which was swept beneath the sea by the gods because of the wickedness of its people. The story of the vanished glories of Atlantis has been used by people who prefer to believe extraordinary reasons for what happens in the world. They have regarded Atlantis as the origin of ancient American civilizations, of flying saucers and of the islanders of the Pacific Ocean. However, some archaeologists have

begun to suggest Plato's tale may contain a grain of truth. In the fifteenth century BC, the island of Thera, 120 kilometres north of Crete, was destroyed by a vast volcanic explosion. There is evidence that the great Minoan civilization of Crete disintegrated at about the same time. It has been suggested that the destruction at the Minoan palace of Knossos was the result of volcanic ash and gases. So Plato's story of Atlantis expresses a dim memory of the fall of Cretan civilization.

Another popular myth is that of buried treasure awaiting rediscovery. One of the most famous of these myths concerns El Dorado – the 'Gilded One'. The first Europeans to reach South America heard tales of the vast golden wealth of one of its rulers. Moving inland, they found many peoples using gold, but never discovered the legendary golden ruler or his capital. By the mid-sixteenth century the myth

This richly carved slab covers the grave of an important Maya priest at Palenque, Mexico. One author believes the figure in the centre is an astronaut in his spaceship. Maya scholars, however, see him simply as a falling figure decked in ceremonial feathers and jade.

Lake Guatavita, Colombia, scene of the El Dorado ritual. The channel in the far shore was cut in one of the first attempts to drain away the water, in order to find the treasure. Below left is the gold model of the raft from which offerings were thrown into Lake Guatavita, during the El Dorado ceremony, about AD 1200.

Legends such as these often develop in the borderland between oral tradition and written history. Stories are passed down from one story-teller to another and the facts become hazy. Such is the legend of King Arthur. After the Romans had withdrawn from Britain in the fifth century AD, the Anglo-Saxon invaders arrived. Some Britons, such as Arthur, returned to the hillforts of their ancestors and held out against them. There is little early written evidence about him. It was the songs of medieval minstrels that turned him into a great romantic hero. Some historians have dismissed him as a complete myth. Others have seen him as a British chieftain, possibly a cavalry leader. Recently, excavations have been carried out at the Iron Age hillfort of Cadbury Castle in Somerset, one of the sites traditionally associated with his capital, Camelot. They revealed that a timber hall with strong defences had been built there in the fifth or sixth century AD. This points to the existence of an important local leader, which fits in with the general picture of the Arthurian legend. Perhaps, after all, Arthur is not just a myth.

Archaeological remains and ruins often give rise to myths themselves, especially when there is apparently no simple explanation for them. Some authors have written at length about extra-terrestrial influences and contacts revealed, for example, by the carving of a 'spaceman' on a Maya tomb at Palenque, Mexico. Archaeologists have found no evidence whatsoever to support this theory and can often explain such 'mysteries' more rationally.

of El Dorado had taken shape. He was a ruler who each year covered himself with gold-dust, and in a great ritual threw many offerings of gold and emeralds into a sacred lake. People searched for this wealth mainly in Lake Guatavita in Colombia. From 1545 onwards, many attempts were made to drain it and recover the supposedly vast treasure it contains. Some gold was found, enough to convince and encourage later treasure hunters. In 1962 the Colombian authorities prohibited further attempts. The lake seems likely to keep its secrets. The truth about the riches of El Dorado will probably remain unknown.

Archaeology and Anthropology

Archaeologists study dead societies. Their work is based on material evidence, which they use to reconstruct the lives of the people who left it behind. Writings, or even paintings and carvings, may tempt them to draw conclusions about the ideas and beliefs of the people who made them. Where such things are lacking, they are forced to concentrate on seeing how the people's environment and technology shaped the pattern of their lives and the structure of their society. Except in a few rare cases, like industrial archaeology, they can never question the people they are studying. But this is what social anthropologists do all the time when they live in so-called primitive societies.

In Mailu, Papua-New Guinea, women still make pots by building up and smoothing together coils of clay.

Aborigines from Central Australia.

Rock and cave paintings, left by the Bushmen, or San, of South Africa and Lesotho, give us a vivid picture of hunter gatherer life.

Anthropologists study living societies, their social life, customs, beliefs and technology, and can watch them change and develop. It is these very characteristics which have determined what Mankind has made and left behind for the archaeologist to discover. Archaeology and anthropology, therefore, are vitally linked.

Archaeologists and anthropologists have worked together in the past. In the last century and the early part of this century, some archaeologists tried to make use of examples drawn from existing 'primitive' peoples to interpret the things they excavated. It was then widely accepted that all societies evolved in the same general way. Societies of the same type, whether living or dead, could be directly compared with each other. It was thought that evidence drawn from the hunting and gathering Australian Aborigines, about their social and religious life, could be used to explain the way of life of Stone Age hunters and gatherers throughout the world. But this idea often led to attributing certain characteristics of one group to another without proper evidence.

As they did more research, anthropologists tended to lay greater stress on how unique each of the tribes was that they studied. Archaeologists realized that comparing prehistoric communities with living societies was of little value if the groups lived in different geographical areas.

Anthropologists studying tribal societies have changed many basic ideas about prehistoric groups. Work on the Bushmen of the Kalahari Desert and the Hadza of Tanzania, for example, has shown that hunting and gathering groups need not necessarily live hard and difficult lives. In fact, they find it comparatively easy to get food and shelter, and even have plenty of free time. Anthropologists have worked in New Guinea where axes and decorative shells are traded over many kilometres. This has suggested how systems of exchanging goods develop over long distances.

Recently, archaeologists and anthropologists have again begun to use living societies to test archaeological theories. For example, they map out how rubbish is deposited around camp sites and how long layers take to accumulate. This would help archaeologists estimate how long a prehistoric society had lived on a particular site. They work out whether the types of houses and the arrangement of buildings in a village can reflect the way the people organized their family lives. Even simple observations may be useful. Anthropologists have noticed that some special pots used in religious ceremonies are never taken out of huts. They last much longer than those which are used daily. This may be why the first type of pot does not appear often in excavations, while sherds of the others are very frequent. The shape of pots used every day may change rapidly as so many are broken. All this evidence serves to warn archaeologists against assuming that all pots in the same layer were made in the same period or had the same life span.

Today both archaeologists and anthropologists are beginning to understand that the study of living and extinct societies cannot be separated. This study of Mankind can only advance if students of both subjects work hand in hand.

Archaeology Today

Archaeology is a new and developing study which has grown rapidly in the last hundred and fifty years. It is a strange mixture of hard manual labour, keen observation, applied science and educated guesswork. This sets it apart from other subjects.

Since the Second World War, it has been revolutionized by scientific discoveries. Radiocarbon and thermoluminescence methods enable us to date sites with astonishing accuracy. Analysis of metals and stone has shown how widespread trading networks were in our distant past and how skilled ancient smiths and miners were. Computers can store unimaginable quantities of information. They can be programmed to produce it in response to many different questions.

Archaeology has become far more scientific. Many chemists, physicists, statisticians, botanists and zoologists are involved in archaeological research. It is vital for archaeologists to understand how scientific specialists can help them build up a fuller picture of prehistoric societies. But it is just as important for them to retain their intuition and imagination in order to give flesh to the dry bones of the excavated past.

Public enthusiasm for archaeology has become very great in the developed countries. Many archaeologists make a special point of explaining new theories and discoveries to a mass audience through television and radio programmes, lectures, exhibitions and magazine articles.

Excavation is a highly skilled job. It must be directed by a trained and experienced archaeologist. But unlike many professions there is still a warm welcome and a place for the amateur. Many museums need voluntary help in cataloguing and sorting their collections. This is one of the best ways of increasing our knowledge of the subject. On excavations, helpers can dig and experience the excitement of unearthing clues which unravel the puzzle of our past. Less active enthusiasts can lend a hand with sorting and cleaning pottery and other remains. Many amateurs enjoy studying archaeology at evening classes and spend holidays on training digs. A considerable number of universities have set up degree courses and each year more professionally trained archaeologists graduate.

There is still so much for them to explore. Air photography has revealed hundreds of intriguing sites in every part of the world. What, for example, is the secret of the gigantic earthen monument, shaped like a jaguar, lying on the eastern flanks of a volcano in the Andes? Who built it? What was its purpose?

Ancient societies may soon be dramatically brought to life when their writings have been decoded. Perhaps when the script carved on wooden boards by the Easter Islanders has been deciphered, we will learn fascinating details about the Polynesian people who raised the enormous stone statues.

In the past twenty years, some scholars have argued that archaeologists must give greater attention to explaining the material they excavate. They must show how this relates to the prehistoric societies that produced it. This movement, often called the New Archaeology, concentrates on economic and social interpretation of finds from the earth, rather than the old-fashioned classification of pots, tools and weapons. The New Archaeologists have again started to use the evidence from anthropological studies in interpreting archaeology. Some theories about prehistoric peoples can be tested by directly observing living, primitive peoples. To many modern archaeologists, therefore, their subject is only part of the wider study of human beings, anthropology.

Dramatic revolutions in climate and economy, wars and peaceful trading links, have shaped and are still shaping our human societies. Both archaeologists and anthropogists are now working together to identify and explain these world-wide forces of change. Such forces have directed our development from the time of *Australopithecus* to the present day.

This air photograph shows the great circular walled city of Firuzabad, Iran, built in the third century AD. Outcrops of the Zagros mountains rise in the background. Much archaeological research remains to be done on this fascinating site.

Glossary

Absolute dating: new scientific dating methods by which archaeologists give their finds precise dates, accurately fixed in time. The principle absolute dating methods used are based on radiocarbon, potassium argon and thermoluminescence tests.

Anatolia: the area which is now called Turkey

Artefact: any object made by human beings

Assyria: an ancient state of Mesopotamia (modern Iraq), which flourished from 1900 to 612 BC

Australopithecus: (means 'Southern ape') the earliest known form of the human type yet found, which lived up to three million years ago

Barrow: a mound of earth and stones raised over a burial

Chalcolithic: (means 'copper and stone') the time when some objects were made of copper, but almost all tools were still made of stone

Classical: refers to the civilizations of ancient Greece and Rome (600 BC to AD 400), their gods, art styles and literature, which formed the basis of education and learning in the West until the present century

Cuneiform: the type of wedge-shaped writing on clay invented in Mesopotamia, and used from 3500 to 500 BC

Dendrochronology: (means 'tree-dating') the science of dating wooden objects by identifying patterns in the annual growth ring of the tree from which the artefact was made

Earthwork: an artificial bank of earth and stone, usually a fortification or for ceremonial purposes

Eolith: (means 'dawn stone') once thought to be the earliest type of stone tool, but now proved to be the result of natural forces of erosion

Feature: used in archaeology to describe things such as walls, pits, post-holes and hearths that are found during excavation

Fossil: ancient animal or plant remains preserved in rocks; usually only the harder parts, such as bones and woody stems, are fossilized

Grave goods: the objects placed in graves and tombs, which were intended to equip the dead person in the afterlife

Hieroglyphs: (means 'sacred carvings') the picture-writing of the ancient Egyptians, used from about 3100 BC, and engraved on temple walls and monuments

Hominid: (from Latin *'homo'*, a man) a member of the family that includes our ape-like ancestors and modern Man

Homo erectus: 'upright man', the third stage in human evolution, had learnt to walk upright. It lived in the Far East and Africa about half a million years ago, and probably spread across most of the Old World

Homo habilis: 'handy man', represents the second stage in human evolution, made the first tools and lived one and a half to half a million years ago

Homo sapiens: 'wise man', represents the latest stage in human evolution

Ideogram: a written sign or symbol that represents an idea

Iberia: the ancient name for the large peninsula that is now divided into the countries of Spain and Portugal

Industrial Revolution: the transformation from agricultural to industrial economies from about AD 1750 in northwestern Europe and North America. This change was helped by numerous inventions such as steam-power.

Inorganic: any material that is not made from a substance which has lived. Stone, clay and metals are the most common inorganic materials.

Mesolithic: (means the 'Middle Stone Age') the period following the last Ice Age, which spanned the gap between the hunting and gathering peoples of the Old Stone Age and the agricultural communities of the New Stone Age

Mesopotamia: (means the 'land between two rivers') the area between the Tigris and Euphrates rivers where some of the world's earliest cities developed; today part of Iraq

Mummy: the body of a dead person, preserved to keep it lifelike

Neanderthal Man: a near relative of modern Man (*Homo sapiens*) which lived 80 000 to 30 000 years ago, and is now extinct

Neolithic: (means the 'New Stone Age') the period when people developed farming, but stone tools were still used

Organic: anything made of substances which have once lived, such as wood, charcoal, peat, bone and antler

Palaeolithic: (means the 'Old Stone Age') the period covering most of Mankind's existence on Earth, from the time of the first tool-making hominids (*Homo-habilis*) to the end of the last Ice Age at about 10 000 BC

Pictograms: the earliest form of writing in which objects are represented by pictures

Postholes: marks in the soil that show where upright timber posts of buildings, onto which walls or roofs were fixed, were set or driven into holes in the ground. The layout of postholes can reveal the plan of a building, and the depth can indicate the height of the posts which they once held. Reconstructions of timber houses are based on this evidence.

Potassium-argon dating: a method of absolute dating, based on the principle of radioactive decay in volcanic rocks

Potsherd: a piece of broken pottery

Proton magnetometer: a machine for measuring small differences in the Earth's magnetic field which reveal buried archaeological remains

Radiocarbon dating: one of the most important scientific methods of dating archaeological finds, based on the principle of the steady decay of radioactive carbon 14 in all organic matter

Ramapithecus: a hominid that lived from about twelve million years ago, and seems to fill the gap between apes and Australopithecus

Section: the vertical side of an excavated trench in which the strata or layers can be seen and studied

Seed machine: a large water tank in which sieved soil is placed and through which air bubbles are then forced, making any organic material, especially small seeds, husks and dried leaves, float to the surface. The plant remains are dried out and studied in order to discover what plants were used by the ancient inhabitants of a site.

Soil resistivity meter: measures differences in the water content of the soil, by passing an electrical current through it to detect, for example, underlying pits and ditches, which retain more moisture than the surrounding soils

Stratification: the way in which rocks, soils, clays, etc., in the earth form layers, the most recent ones lying on top of the earlier ones. The stratification of ancient sites is often complicated since the layers are sometimes mixed up and patchy. As excavation proceeds the archaeologist must study, record and interpret the stratigraphy with great care.

Sumeria: an area of southern Mesopotamia where civilization first began at about 3500 BC

Thermoluminescence: (means 'giving out light when heated') a scientific dating method based on the fact that when pottery is heated, it will give out light that can be measured. The more light that is given out, the older the pot or baked clay object.

Index

Acknowledgements

The publishers gratefully acknowledge permission to reproduce the following illustrations:

Aerofilms Ltd. 71l; Ancient Monuments Laboratory: Crown Copyright reserved 21, 25; University of Arizona, Laboratory of Tree Ring Research 29; Aspect Picture Library Ltd 38; A-Z Botanical Collection Ltd 28; David Baerreis 61t; Iris Barry 89b; Barnaby's Picture Library 49, 64; Tom Blagg/Trinity School Models 71r; Warwick Bray 58t; BBC Copyright 80; Courtesy of the Trustees of the British Museum 7t, 18br, 23, 26, 32, 37t, 39b, 47l, 48, 57l, 59, 65tr, 66, 67b, 70r, 73b, 81, 82b, 87tc, tr; Camelot Research Committee 13; Peter Clayton 18bl, 21, 37b, 53, 57r, 68t, 69, 73tr, 79, 85bl; Bruce Coleman Ltd. 15l; Colorific 43, 90r; Daily Telegraph Colour Library 55; Robert Estall Photographs 11, 17r, 27, 41tl; C. von Fürer-Haimendorf 51b; Georg Gerster/John Hillelson Agency 93; Griffith Museum 75b; Susan Griggs Agency Ltd. 85br, 87tl, br, 88, 89t; Gerald H. Grosso 18tr, 19t; Robert Harding Associates 12; Hans Hinz 51t; The Illustrated London News 72; G. J. Irwin 90l; P. R. Jones/Laetoli Research Project 47r; Carol Kane 41r; Keystone Press Agency Ltd. 16, 17l, 19b, 74; City of Liverpool Museums 1; Livingstone Museum, Zambia 68b; The Mansell Collection 8, 9, 35l, 40, 56, 62, 67t, 70l, 73tl, 77, 78, 84, 85t; Museum of London/Department of Urban Archaeology 14, 15tr, 63b; National Monuments Air Photograph: Crown Copright reserved 10; Peabody Museum/Harvard University 82t; Ann and Bury Peerless 34; Photoresources 75t; John Picton 33t; Pictorial Colour Slides 41bl, 61b; Picturepoint Ltd. 31, 83; Popperphoto 24b; Josephine Powell 54; Dr P. J. Reynolds/Butser Ancient Farm Project 45; Department of Information Production Services, Rhodesia 65b; Royal Anthropological Institute of Great Britain and Ireland 24t; Royal Institute of the Tropics, Amsterdam 73tc; St Louis Art Museum 6; Salisbury and South Wiltshire Museum 7b; Scottish Tourist Board 76; Chosuke Serisawa, Tokoku 58b; Thames & Hudson Ltd. 63t; Roger Viollet 33l, 65tl; Wasavarvet/Sjöhoriska museet, Stockholm 39t; York Archaeological Trust 35r.

Jacket photographs: front, Susan Griggs Agency Ltd.; back, Barnaby's Picture Library

Artwork by: Linda Broad 23, 25, 44, 50, 62, 79, 86–7; Martin Causer 60; Michael Craig 46, 48, 53, 76–7; James Roper 22, 46, 55, 56; Swanston & Associates 8, 20, 52, 54; Technical Art Services 26, 29, 30, 31, 36.